Persia Revisited

Thomas Edward Gordon

Contents

PERSIA REVISITED

BY

Thomas Edward Gordon

PREFACE

On revisiting Tehran last autumn, I was struck with the evidence of progress and improvement in Persia, and on returning home I formed the idea of publishing a short account of my journey, with observations and opinions which are based on my previous experiences, and have reference also to what has been recorded by others. In carrying out this idea, I have made use of information given in the well-known books on Persia by Malcolm, Fraser, Watson and Curzon.

'Persia Revisited,' as first written, comprised up to Chapter VI. of the book; but just as I had finished it for publication, the sad news of the assassination of the Shah, Nasr-ed-Din, was received. I then saw that my book, to be complete, should touch on the present situation in Persia, and accordingly I added two chapters which deal with the new Shah and his brothers, and the Sadr Azem and the succession.

The illustrations are from photographs by M. Sevragine of Tehran, with the exception of the likeness of H.I.M. the Shah Mozuffer-ed-Din, and that of H.H. Ali Asghar Khan, Sadr Azem, which latter, by Messrs. W. and D. Downey, of Ebury Street, London, is published by their kind permission.

T.E. GORDON.
May, 1896.

PERSIA REVISITED
CHAPTER I.

--London to Baku --Oil-wells and works --Persians abroad --Caspian steamers --Caspian salmon --Enzelli lagoon --The Jews in Persia --Resht trade --'My eye' --Russian road --The tobacco 'strike,' 1891 --Collapse of Tobacco Regie --Moulla opposition.

The Persians, as a people still nomadic in their habits, and much given to long pilgrimages, have good knowledge of the ways and means of making a journey pleasant. Their saying, 'Avval rafik, baad tarik' (First a companion, then the road), is one which most travellers can fully appreciate. Accordingly, when planning a trip in the autumn of 1895 to the Land of Iran, I cast about for a companion, and was fortunate enough to meet with two friends, both going that way, and who, moreover, like myself, had previously journeyed in Persia.

We decided to take the Odessa route to Batoum, and we went by Berlin, Oderberg, and Lemberg. At Odessa we found that a less expensive, and more comfortable, though perhaps half a day longer route, lies by Warsaw. On that line there are fewer changes, and only one Customs examination, whereas by, Oderberg there are two examinations, Austrian and Russian. Moreover, through tickets are issued *via* Warsaw, a convenience not provided *via* Oderberg--fresh tickets and re-booking of luggage being necessary there, and again both at Pod Voloczyska and Voloczyska, on the Austrian and Russian frontiers. We came in for a crowded train of first-class passengers going from the Vienna direction to Jalta, a favourite seaside place in the Crimea, which has two fashionable seasons--spring and autumn. These people were making for the accelerated mail-steamer, which leaves Odessa for Batoum every Wednesday during the summer service, touching at Sebastopol, Jalta, and Novorossisk. We were making for the same steamer, and found crowded cabins. The mass of luggage to be examined at Voloczyska caused much confusion and delay, and it was only by discreetly managed appeals to the working staff that we were able to push our way and pass on, without anything being left behind. There appeared to be orders for very special examination of books and papers at Voloczyska, and these were carried out in a foolishly perfunctory manner. In my luggage, the man who searched passed over a bulky tourist writing-case, but carried off to a superior a Continental Bradshaw, a blank notebook, and a packet of useful paper, notwithstanding my open show of their innocence. The man soon returned with another official, who smiled at the mistake, and good naturedly helped to close up my baggage.

We began our journey well by a rapid run to Odessa, arriving there on the day of departure of the fast boat, and landing at Batoum in six and a half days from London. The steamers on this service are about 2,500 tons, 2,400 horse-power, with large accommodation for passengers. The cabins are comfortable, and the saloons excellent and well served, and all are lit with the electric light. These boats are, I believe, Tyne-built. They are broad of beam, and behave well in bad weather. Novorossisk is a growing great port, situated in a very pretty bay. It has lately been joined by railway to the main trunk line connecting with Moscow, and passing through Rostov. This connection enables it to attract considerable trade from the Don and the Volga, and also to take much from Rostov and Taganrog, when the Azov approaches are closed with ice. A very fine sea-wall, to give effectual protection to the railway loading-piers, and the shipping generally, is now being completed at a total cost of L850,000. Novorossisk is said to have the biggest 'elevator' in the world. The scenery all along the coast, from the Crimea to Batoum, is very fine, and in autumn the voyage is most enjoyable.

We left Batoum on the night of the day of our arrival. The departure of the through train to Baku had been changed from morning to night, and this allowed of travelling by day over that part of the line which before used to be passed at night. We had previously seen Tiflis, and therefore did not break our journey. The weather was warm, but not such as to cause discomfort. As we approached Tiflis the carriages and buffets became crowded to excess, with townspeople returning from Saturday-to-Monday holiday, the fine weather having enticed them out to various places along the line. The railway-carriages on the Batoum-Baku line are very comfortable, and the refreshment-rooms are frequent and well provided, so travelling there is made easy and pleasant. The journey occupies thirty-two hours.

We reached Baku on September 16, the ninth day from London, and arranged to leave for Enzelli, on the Persian coast, the port for Tehran, at midnight the next day. Through the kindness of a member of the Greek house of Kousis, Theophylactos and Co., we were shown over the oil-wells and refineries belonging to M. Taghioff, a millionaire of Persian origin (the name probably was Taghi Khan). The story goes that, on becoming wealthy through the oil industry in its early days, he presented the young township with a church, school-house, and hospital, and, in recognition of his generous public spirit, the Government gave him a grant of the waste land on which his works now stand, and out of which millions of roubles have come to him from oil-springs. Our visit had the appearance of bringing him luck in the form of a new fountain rush. We had seen all the works and wells; none of the latter were flowing, and the usual steam-pumping was going on. We were about to leave, when a commotion at the wells attracted our attention, and we saw the dark fluid spouting up from two to three hundred feet through the open top of the high-peaked wooden roof erected over each of the wells. On hurrying back, we saw the great iron cap, which is swung vertically when the pump is working, lowered and fixed at some height over the mouth of the well, to drive the outward flow down into the hollow all round and out into the ditch leading to the reservoirs. The force of the gush was shown by the roar of the dash against the iron cap, and the upward rush had the appearance of a solid quivering column. The flow was calculated at fifty thousand gallons an hour. The business of refining is generally in the hands of others than the producers; but some of the larger firms--notably the Rothschilds, Nobel Brothers, and Taghioff--are both producers and refiners. This means of course, the employment of very, much larger capital.

There is a great dash of the gambling element in the oil-well business at Baku. Large sums are spent in boring operations, and success so often stands off that all available capital is sunk in the ground and swallowed up. Even with good signs, it is impossible to foresee the results or the extent of production, and there is also an extraordinary irregularity in the outcome of the separate naphtha-bearing plots. An instance was mentioned to me of a peasant proprietor who had made enough money on which to live sumptuously, but he hungered for more, and engaged in further boring operations. He was on the verge of losing everything, when oil was suddenly struck, and he made a fortune. He laboured hard himself, and literally went to sleep a poor working man, and awoke to find his dream of riches realized.

Baku has been immensely improved in every way of late, and now has good streets, hotels, and shops. Water, which was a great want before, is well supplied from condensers which belong to the town. The rise in the value of house property and building sites within the last ten years has been enormous, and great part of the money thus made has gone to native owners, Persians (or Tartars, as all Mohammedans are called here), and I was told of a plot of building ground with a small house on it, which had been originally bought for 600 roubles, being lately sold for 30,000. The town is growing in size, and new buildings are rising, which give an appearance of prosperity and increasing trade. The harbour is crowded with steamers and sailing vessels, and the wharfs present a busy sight. The loading and unloading is quickly done by steam-cranes and powerful porters, who come in numbers from the Persian districts of Khalkhal and Ardabil. I watched with much interest a gang of these men at work. They were wonderfully quick, quiet, and methodical in their ways, and showed great capacity for handling and carrying heavy weights.

Baku swarms with Persians, resident and migratory. They are seen everywhere--as shopkeepers, mechanics, masons, carpenters, coachmen, carters, and labourers, all in a bustle of business, so different from Persians, at home. Climate or want of confidence produces indolence there, but here and elsewhere out of Persia they show themselves to be active, energetic, and very intelligent. They are in great numbers at all the censes of trade in the adjoining countries--at Constantinople, Damascus, Aleppo, Baghdad, Tiflis, Askhabad, and other towns. Most of the new buildings in Tiflis were built by Persians, and thousands were engaged in the construction of the Trans-Caspian Railway. The permanent workmen now employed on it are largely Persians, and Askhabad has a resident population of over twelve thousand. There were said to be twenty thousand Persians, from the provinces of Azerbaijan and Hamadan, working last summer on the new railway from Tiflis to Alexandropol and Kars, now being built, and doubtless many of them will permanently settle on the line.

It is said that there are half a million thus located and working out of Persia, but I think that this is an exaggerated estimate. Most of them retain their nationality, for while they grumble loudly in their own country, yet when away they swear by it, and save money steadily to enable them to return home. Their nomadic character is the cause of this readiness to seek employment abroad. I was told that in 1894-95 twenty thousand Persian passports were issued from the Embassy in Constantinople. This would include pilgrims as well as home visitors. It is this love of country (not in the sense, however, of patriotism as understood in the West) which makes a Persian cling to his national representative abroad, and willingly pay for frequent registration as a subject who is entitled to protection and permission to return home whenever he may choose. As a rule, the Persian abroad always appears in the distinctive national dress--the tall black lambskin cap and the coat with ample skirt of many pleats.

I have mentioned the Persian porters who are seen at Baku; they are also to be found at Petrovsk and Astrachan, and are generally preferred to the local labourers, who, in common with their class in Russia, take a long drink once a week, often unfitting them for their work the following day. The Persians are of sober habits, and can be relied upon for regular attendance at the wharfs and loading-stages. They have learnt, however, to take an occasional taste of the *rakivodka* spirit, and when reminded that they are Mohammedans, say that the indulgence was prohibited when no one worked hard. These porters are men of powerful physique, and display very great strength in bearing separate burdens; but they cannot work together and make a joint effort to raise heavy loads, beyond the power of one man. Singly, they are able to lift and carry eighteen poods, Russian weight, equal to six hundred and forty-eight pounds English.

In the newspaper correspondence on the burning Armenian Question, I have seen allusion made to the poor physique of the Armenian people; but as far as my observation goes in Persia, Russian Armenia, and the Caucasus, there is no marked difference between them and the local races, and on the railway between Baku and Tiflis Armenian porters of powerful form are common, where contract labour rates attract men stronger than their fellows.

Though much of the wealth which has come out of the Baku oil-fields has been carried away by foreign capitalists, yet much remains with the inhabitants, and the investment of this has promoted trade in the Caspian provinces, and multiplied the shipping. There are now between one hundred and eighty and two hundred steamers on the Caspian, besides a large number of sailing craft of considerable size, in which German and Swedish, as well as Armenian and Tartar-Persian, capital is employed. The Volga Steam Navigation Company is divided into two companies-- one for the river, and the other for the Caspian. The latter owns six large steamers, with cargo capacity of from sixty to eighty thousand poods, liquid measurement, for oil-tank purposes, equalling nine hundred to twelve hundred tons. They have German under-officers, and Russian captains. It is likely that the German officers come from the German colonies on the Volga, and probably some of the capital also comes from that quarter. This Volga Steam Navigation Company was established over fifty years ago by a Scotchman, named Anderson, and some of the vessels first built are still used on the river as cargo-boats.

Many of the best steamers on the Caspian are officered by Swedes and Finns, most of whom speak English, acquired whilst serving in English ships sailing to all parts of the globe. The Mercury Company, which runs the superior steamers and carries the mails on the Caspian, has Swedish and Finn officers, but it is said that they are now to be replaced by Russian naval officers as vacancies occur. This company's vessels are well appointed, have good cabins, and are fitted with the electric light. But the best of Caspian mail-boats are most uncomfortable in rough weather for all but those whom no motion whatever can affect. Owing to the shoal water on all the coast circumference of this sea, the big boats are necessarily keelless, and may be described as but great barges with engines, and when at anchor in a rolling sea their movement is terribly disturbing.

We embarked in the Admiral Korneiloff, one of the Mercury Company's best boats, on the night of September 17, and arrived at Enzelli on the morning of the 19th. I was amused on the voyage to hear the sailors' version of the story how the Caspian became a Russian sea, on which no armed Persian vessel can sail. The sovereignty of this Persian sea was ceded to Russia by the Treaty of Gulistan in 1813, and the sailors say that on the Shah being pressed over and over again to consent, and desiring to find some good excuse to do so, a courtier, seeing the royal inclination, remarked that Persia suffered sorely from salt soil and water, which made land barren, and that sea-water was of no use for irrigation, nor any other good purpose. The Shah on this asked if it were really true that the water of the Caspian was salt, and on being assured that it was, he said the Russians might have the whole of it.

We found an improvement at Enzelli in the form of a hotel kept by a Greek, with accommodation good enough to be very welcome. We had excellent fresh salmon at breakfast, which reminded me of the doubt that has often been expressed of the true salmon being found in an inland sea. The Caspian fish is a genuine salmon of the same habits as the marine species known in Europe, with the one sad exception that it will not look at nor touch fly or bait in any form or shape, and therefore gives no sport for the rod. The trout in the upper waters of the streams that the salmon run up, take the fly freely and give good sport, but all attempts by keen and clever fishermen to hook a salmon have failed. The fish are largely netted, and same are sent to Tehran packed in ice, while a good business is done in salting what cannot be sold fresh. The existence of salmon in this inland salt sea, which lies eighty-four feet below the level of the ocean, is supposed to be due to its connection with the open sea having been cut off by a great upheaval in the prehistoric time.

After breakfast we were confronted with a functionary new to us in Persia, one charged with the demand for passports and their examination. He is prepared to provide passports for those arriving without them, and to *vise* when this has not been previously done. Considering the practice in force with Persia's near neighbour, and the crowd of deck-passengers always coming and going, it was not likely that this formality as a source of income would fail to be adopted. The linguistic educational qualification for the post is evidently confined to Russian, for on finding that I spoke Persian, the officer asked me for the information he pretended to seek from the English passports. He acknowledged the farce he was called upon to play, and we proceeded without any farther inquiry. The day was warm, but not oppressively so; the sea-breeze helped the boat across the lagoon and up the Pir-i-Bazaar stream, and the weather being dry, we reached Resht in carriages By the Mobarakabad route, without the splashing plunging through a sea of mud which is the general disagreeable experience of the main road.

The Enzelli Lagoon is a swarming haunt of numerous kinds of wild-fowl and fishing birds. Conspicuous among the waders in the shallows and on the shore are the pelican and the stork. The place is a paradise to them, teeming with fish and frog food. One of my companions described what he had witnessed in a struggle with a wounded stork in the shallow water of this lagoon. He and a friend were out after wild-duck, and his friend, desiring to bag a giant stork, which looked splendid in his strongly contrasted pure white and deep black plumage, fired, and wounded the bird. His Persian servant, with thoughts intent on cooking it, ran, knife in hand, to cut its throat in the orthodox manner, so as to make it lawful for a Mohammedan to eat. The bird, on being seized, struggled hard with its captor, and, snapping its elongated bill widely in wild terror, by accident got the man's head jammed between its mandibles. The keen cutting edges of the long strong beak scarified the man's cheeks, and made him scream with pain and with frantic fear that it was *his* throat which was being cut. His master went to his assistance and released him by wrenching open the stork's bill, but he was so occupied with supporting his swooning servant that time was given for the wounded stork to hurry away in safety, flapping its long wings and snapping its powerful beak, as is the habit of this voiceless bird, with all the appearance of triumph.

Enzelli is becoming the port of entry, for the North of Persia, of tea from India and China. Till within a very short time most of the tea for Persia, Trans-Caspia, and Russian Turkistan so far as Samarkand, passed up from Bombay by the Persian Gulf ports. The late reduction in Russian railway charges, and the low sea-freights from the East in the oil-steamers returning to Batoum, have brought about this change. Arrangements have been made for transit to Baku of Russian-owned tea consigned to Persia on special terms of Customs drawback, and it is now sold cheaper in Resht than in Baku, where it has a heavy duty added to the price. The thin muslin-like manufactures of India, in demand in Central Asia for wear in the hot dry summer, and which found their way there from the Persian Gulf, are now following the same route as the tea. Thus, steam and waterway are competing still more with the camel, to make the longest way round the shortest one in point of time, and the cheapest to the customers' homes.

As with tea, so Russian beet-sugar is cheaper at Enzelli-Resht than at Baku, owing to the State bounty on export. The consumption of tea and sugar, already large in Persia, is certain to increase in the North through this development of Russian trade. French beet-sugar continues to compete by way of Trebizond to Tabriz, but if the experiment now being tried of manufacturing sugar in the vicinity of Tehran from beet succeeds, the Persians will benefit further by competition.

The Russian trade in Persia is mostly in the hands of Armenians, some of whom have amassed considerable wealth. It is only in the West that the Jew is regarded as the sample of superior sharpness in the walks of life that call for the exercise of the qualities most necessary in the operation of getting the better of one's neighbour. In the East both the Greek and the Armenian are ahead of him in this respect, and the popular saying is, 'One Greek equals two Jews, and one Armenian equals two Greeks.' But, to the credit of the Armenian traders, it should be said that they are bold and enterprising in a newly-opened country, as well as clever in an old one. It may be here mentioned that there is no opening in Persia for the native Jew; he is there refused the facilities which lead to wealth, and is strictly confined to the poorest occupations. It is not unlikely that the severe treatment of the Jews in Persia has its origin in the hatred inspired by the conduct of Saad-u-Dowleh, a Jewish physician, who rose to the position of Supreme Vazir under the King Arghoun Khan, in 1284. This Minister owed his advancement to his pleasing manners and agreeable conversation, and he gained such an ascendancy over his weak royal master as to be allowed to remove all Mohammedans from places of trust and profit, and even to carry his persecution to the length of commanding that no one professing that faith should appear at Court. The Eastern Christians were then much more prominent and numerous than they afterwards became, and Saad-u-Dowleh sank his people's dislike of the Nazarene in his greater hate of the Mohammedan, so that he employed the former to replace the followers of the Arabian Prophet whom he dismissed from office and banished from Court. The penalty of death was exacted for this persecution, for Saad-u-Dowleh was murdered almost at the same instant that his sovereign master expired.

The silk trade of Resht, which has suffered so much for many years from the disease that attacked the silkworms in the Caspian provinces, and spread to all the Persian silk districts, is now recovering. The introduction of cellular seed has been attended with much success, and there is a rapidly-increasing export of cocoons. The fresh start in this old industry has given an impetus to mulberry-tree cultivation, and waste land is in considerable demand for planting purposes.

An attempt is now being made to grow tea on the low hills near Batoum. It is not yet known what may be the ultimate chances of success, but already what is being done there is having the effect of suggesting a similar experiment near Resht. The conditions of the soil on many of the wooded hill-slopes in the Persian Caspian provinces, where every gradation of climate and atmosphere can be met with, appear to be well adapted for the tea-plant. The cart-road to Kasvin, now being constructed by a Russian company, will pass through some of these well-favoured parts, and this will help to draw attention to natural resources which have hitherto been unnoticed.

As old Persian travellers, we were at once reminded of our return to the land of complimentary address and extravagant phrase by the frequent reply '*Chashm*' (My eye!), the simple slang expression known in our country, and which 'Trilby' has made better known by its introduction on the stage. The word is an abbreviation of 'Ba sar o chashm' (By my head and eyes! May my eyes be put out, and my head taken off, if I obey not!). We also heard the similar but less formal reply *Chira*? Why?--meaning, why not? why should I not do as you desire? i.e. you will be obeyed.

We travelled to Kasvin, halfway to Tehran, over the execrable road which leads from Resht. For the first forty miles the landscape was lovely from wooded slopes, green growth and clear running water. The post-houses are just as they were--ill-provided, and affording the very smallest degree of comfort that it is possible for a 'rest-house' to give. They had been in some way improved for the reception of General Prince Karaupatkin, and his suite, who visited Tehran to announce to the Shah the accession of H.I.M. Nicolas II.; but no effort to maintain the improvement had been made, except in one place--Menzil. The on dit in Tehran was, that the successful launching of the Russian cart-road enterprise, now fairly well in hand, is entirely due to Prince Karaupatkin's strong representation on his return to St. Petersburg. He is said to have taken the opportunity of telling the Shah, in answer as to his journey up, that he was greatly surprised to find the road leading to the capital such a very bad one; whereupon his Majesty remarked that the blame lay with his own countrymen, who, after begging for a monopoly concession to construct a good road, had held on to it and done nothing, and they had the right, so long as the contract time allowed, to prevent others from making the road. The Russian press, which interested itself in the matter, pointed out that what was wanted to give an impetus to their trade in North Persia was good roads, not bounties, and it may be that the interest which is believed to be guaranteed by the Government on the road capital will take the place of trade bounties. The money subscribed is sufficient to provide a solidly-built road, and the idea is that it will be aligned so as to be fit for railway purposes in the future. The existing cart-road from Kasvin to Tehran is but a track, lined out fairly straight over a level bit of high-lying country, with a few bridges over small streams. The distance, ninety-five miles, is comfortably covered in fourteen to eighteen hours in carriages drawn by three horses. The nature of the ground makes this road a good fair-weather one, and as the Russian company has rented it from the Persian concessionnaire, we may expect to hear of considerable improvements, so as to encourage an increase of the Persian waggon traffic which already exists on it. The completion of a system of quick communication between the Russian Caspian Sea base and the capital of Persia must attract the practical attention of all who are interested in Persian affairs.

Many of the Moullas, in their character as meddlers, are always ready to step forward in opposition to all matters and measures in which they have not been consulted and conciliated. So the Russian road from Resht was pronounced to be a subject for public agitation by the Tabriz Mujtahid, Mirza Javad Agha, who, since his successful contest over the Tobacco Regie, has claimed to be one of the most important personages in Persia. This priest is very rich, and is said to be personally interested in trade and 'wheat corners' at Tabriz, and as he saw that the new road was likely to draw away some of the Tabriz traffic, he set himself the task of stirring up the Moullas of Resht to resent, on religious grounds, the extended intrusion of Europeans into their town. The pretence of zeal in the cause was poor, because the Resht Moullas are themselves interested in local prosperity, and the agitation failed.

A change is coming over the country in regard to popular feeling towards priestly interference in personal and secular affairs. The claim to have control of the concerns of all men may now be said to be but the first flush of the fiery zeal of divinity students, fresh from the red-hot teachings of bigoted Moulla masters, who regret the loss of their old supremacy, and view with alarm the spread of Liberalism, which seems now to be establishing itself in Persia.

The unfortunate episode of the Tobacco Regie in 1891 gave the Moullas a chance to assert themselves, and they promptly seized the opportunity to champion a popular cause of discontent, and the pity of it was that the enterprise which raised the disturbance was English. This tobacco monopoly had been pictured as a business certain to produce great gains, and the people were thus prepared for the reports which were spread of high prices to be charged on what they regard as almost a necessary of life. The conditions of the country were not fully studied before the monopoly powers were put in force. A suggestion was made that the company's operations should be confined at first to the foreign export, which would have returned a good profit, and that afterwards a beginning should be made at Tehran, to prove to the people that the monopoly would really give them better tobacco, and not raise prices, which the company claimed would be the result of their system. But everything was planned on an extensive scale, and so were prospective profits. The picture of a rapid road to fortune had been exhibited, and it was therefore decided that the full right of monopoly should be established at once. An imprudent beginning was made in exercising the right of search in a manner which alarmed some people for the privacy of their homes, a dangerous suggestion in a Mohammedan community.

The suspicions and fears of all--buyers, sellers, and smokers--were easily worked upon by the priests, ever ready to assert the supremacy of the Church over the State. And then the biggest 'strike' I know of took place. Mirza Hassan, the High-Priest of Kerbela, the most sacred shrine of the Shiah Mohammedans, declared tobacco in Persia to be 'unlawful' to the true believer, and everyone--man, woman, and child--was forbidden to sell or smoke it. The 'strike' took place on a gigantic scale, a million or two certainly being engaged in it, and steps were taken to see the order from Kerbela carried out rigorously. 'Vigilance men,' under the Moullas' directions, made raids on suspected tea-shops, to find and smash the 'kalian' pipes which form part of the stock-in-trade of these places of refreshment. The Shah was faced with the sight of silent and forsaken tea-shops as he passed through the streets of Tehran, and he saw the signs of the censuring strike in the rows of empty benches, on which his subjects used to sit at their simple enjoyment of pipes and tea. The interdiction reached the inner homes of all, and even in the *anderuns* and boudoirs of the highest (all of which are smoking-rooms) it was rigidly obeyed. The priestly prohibition penetrated to the palaces, and royalty found authority set at defiance in this matter. A princely personage, a non-smoker, is said to have long urged and entreated a harem favourite, too deeply devoted to tobacco, to moderate her indulgence in it, but to no effect. On the strike being ordered, she at once joined it, and his Highness is reported to have said, 'My entreaties were in vain, my bribes of jewels were refused, yet the priest prevails.' And this was at a place where not long before Moullas had been at a discount.

There are now signs of the people resenting the arrogant assumption or power by the Moullas, and freeing themselves from their thraldom. There has always been great liberty of opinion and speech in Persia, and six hundred years ago the poets Khayyam and Hafiz took full advantage of this in expressing their contempt for the 'meddling Moullas.' Not very long ago the donkey-boys in one of the great towns would on occasion reflect the popular feeling by the shout 'Br-r-r-o akhoond!' (Go on, priest!) when they saw a Moulla pattering along on his riding donkey. **Biro** is Persian for 'go on,' and, rolled and rattled out long and loud, is the cry when droves of load-carrying donkeys are driven. The donkey-boy in Persia is as quick with bold reply as he is in Egypt and elsewhere. There is a story that a high Persian official called out to a boy, whose gang of burden-bearing donkeys obstructed his carriage, 'Out of the way, ass, you driver of asses!' and was promptly answered, 'You are an ass yourself, though a driver of men!'

As a finish to this reference to the Tobacco Regie in Persia, I may mention it is believed that, had the company started as ordinary traders, they, having the command of ready money, would have succeeded well. The commencement made in the centres of tobacco cultivation impressed the peasant producers most favourably; they appreciated the advantages of cash payments, and regretted the cessation of the system, and the governors benefited by the readiness with which the taxes were paid. But the explanation of monopoly, a word which was then unknown in Persia, raised the fears of the people, and those who had the money to spare laid in a supply of tobacco before the concession came into force. This was regarded by the poor as proof of the coming rise in price, and they therefore hailed the Moullas as their deliverers from the threatened calamity of dear tobacco.

The only public debt of Persia is that of a loan contracted in order to pay the compensation for cancelment of this concession, and the expenses which had been incurred; but the sale by the Government of the foreign export (part of the cancelled concession) very nearly provides for the loan. The Societe de 'Tombac' of

Constantinople, which bought the monopoly of export, has had difficulties to contend with, caused by a Persian combination to buy from the cultivators and sell to the foreign agents. A prominent Moulla was named as interested in this business, which was in reality at direct variance with the principles on which the priesthood had declared the original concession to be 'unlawful.' This interference with the free trade conditions existing when the Constantinople company made its contract led to a dispute, which ended with a fresh agreement, in which there is said to be a stipulation that, should the Persian Tobacco Regie in its original form be revived at any time, French subjects are to have the first offer.

After disposing of the Tobacco Regie, the triumphant Moullas desired to extend their prohibition to all foreign enterprise in Persia, and they pronounced against the English Bank, which was doing its work quietly, and without detriment to the business of others. But the Shah gave them clearly to understand that their pretensions would be permitted no further, and that they were to cease from troubling. They then made an attempt to establish the impression of their power in a visible sign on all men, by commanding discontinuance of the Persian fashion of shaving the chin, so that the beard should be worn in accordance with Mohammedan custom. Again they talked of organizing coercion gangs, to enforce the order on the barbers, under threat of wrecking their shops. At this time a foreign diplomat, during an audience of the Shah, on being asked by his Majesty, according to his wont, what news there was in the European quarter of the town, mentioned this latest phase of Moulla agitation as tending to unsettle men's minds. The Shah passed his hand lightly over his shaven chin, and said, with a touch of humour and royal assurance: 'See, I shave; let them talk; they can do nothing.'

It is wrong to suppose that the people of Persia are dead to all desire for progress, and that their religion is a bar to such desire. It is not so. Many of the Moullas, it is true, are opposed to education and progress. One frankly said of the people in reference to education, 'They will read the Koran for themselves, and what will be left for us to do?' The country is advancing in general improvement, slowly, but yet moving forward; not standing still or sliding back, as some say. The Moulla struggles in 1891-92 to gain the upper hand produced a feeling of unquiet, and the most was made of all grievances, so as to fan the flames of discontent. Pestilent priests paraded the country, and did their utmost to excite religious fanaticism against the

Government. These agitators spoke so loudly and rashly that the ire of the old religious leaders, the higher Moullas, men of learning and tranquil temper, who had not joined the party of retrogression, was roused. The knowledge of this emboldened the sober-minded to speak out against the arrogance and conceit of the new self-elected leaders. Open expression of opinion led to the criticism, 'These priests will next desire to rule over us.' The Nomads, who have always declined to be priest-ridden, also showed that they were ready to resist any attempts to establish a religious supremacy in temporal affairs; and then, by judicious management of rival jealousies and conflicting interests, the Shah succeeded in his policy of complete assertion of the royal power. It may be that the Moullas were made to understand that, just as the Chief Priest had risen at a great assembly before Nadir Shah, and advised him to confine himself to temporal affairs, and not to interfere in matters of religion, so similar sound advice in the reverse order was given for their guidance.

CHAPTER II

--The late Shah's long reign --His camp life --Habits --Appearance --Persian Telegraph Intelligence Department --Farming the revenues --Condition of the people --The shoe question --The customs --Importation of arms --Martini-Henry rifles --Indo-European telegraph

Nasr-ed-din Shah was the two hundred and fifty-fourth Sovereign who had successively ascended the throne of Persia. He succeeded his father, Mahomed Shah, on September 10, 1848, and would have entered on his jubilee, the fiftieth year of his reign, according to the Mohammedan calendar, on May 6, 1896, had not his life been suddenly cut short by a dastardly assassin on Friday, May 1. This was, I think, the longest reign of any Persian monarch that can be ascertained with historical accuracy, except that of Shah Tamasp, who died A.D. 1576, after occupying the throne for fifty-three years; but this credits him with having begun his reign at the age of ten years. Nasr-ed-Din Shah ascended the throne at the age of seventeen. Up to the last his Majesty was remarkable as retaining all his physical and mental energies; his health was excellent, due no doubt to his love of nomadic life and its simple habits. He was passionately fond of the chase, and passed much of his time in the saddle. It might well be said of him, as of the ancient Persian monarchs, that the royal edicts were written 'at the stirrup of the King,' for his Ministers had to follow him into the camp and the hunting-field, and this prevented his Court becoming lapped in luxury. Large tracts were preserved for him for ibex and moufflon on the mountains, and antelope on the plains, and the hawking of duck or partridge on by-days. This nomadic life, with its hunting habits, encouraged the pleasant, easy manner which attracted his subjects and commanded their confidence. He was an energetic worker, and had full knowledge of all home and foreign affairs. He was superior to all palace intrigues, if any existed, and his Ministers were rarely changed. The long continuance in office of his councillors added to the feeling of public security which his own strong personality had given to the country.

In appearance Nasr-ed-Din Shah was little changed since 1889, when his figure was a well-known one in Europe. He showed the same alertness of step, brightness of look and manner, and smartness of dress, which distinguished him then. In his Court he was a striking figure, in marked contrast to those about him, for it must be confessed that all in attendance showed some neglect of appearance which compared unfavourably with the tout ensemble of their Sovereign. This may possibly have been a subtle form of flattery, so that the Shah alone might catch the eye and be the 'observed of all observers'--'le Roi-Soleil'--of the land of the Lion and the Sun.

No one probably saw more clearly than the Shah that the system of farming out the administration of the provinces from year to year is bad, both for the Treasury and the people; but he knew well that reform, to be sure and certain, must be slow and gradual, for change in Persia, with its ancient traditions and old memories, cannot be effected at one stroke. He had done much to mitigate the evil of the present system by establishing telegraphic communication with all the centres of provincial government, thus placing himself in close touch with his subjects, even in the most remote parts. Gradually the confidence which began in his near neighbourhood had extended throughout the country, and there was a firm belief in the minds of the people that the Shah could be approached by all. But it can well be imagined that it takes a desperate case to induce those who are oppressed in distant places to have recourse to such a public mode of communicating grievances as the telegraph. Yet the telegraph is so employed at times, the senders of the telegrams giving their names openly, and confidently awaiting the result.

The Persian Telegraph Department has a peculiar importance in being the secret agency by which the Shah is served with an independent and reliable daily report of all that goes on throughout the country. The system of direct reports of the conduct of governors, by special resident officials, which was established in the days of Darius the King, has developed into the present secret service daily telegrams. Nominations to all the telegraph appointments are made by the Minister in charge of the department, who bears the appropriate title of Mukbir-i-Dowleh (Intelligencer of the State).

An instance of the power exercised through this system occurred within my personal knowledge a few years ago. A local dignitary in a distant province fell under the frown of the Prince Governor, who, actuated by greed, imposed on him a heavy fine for an imaginary offence. The fine was not paid, on which a charge of contumacy was made, and this was punished by the cruel bastinado and imprisonment. The Telegraph-master, notwithstanding the fact of the Governor being a near relative of the late Shah, reported the circumstance in all its details. The telegraph enabled the Shah to make his presence felt in distant places, as well as his power, for he was in the habit of occasionally summoning a Governor to the office at the other end of the wire, to hear his commands spoken on the spot. In this instance the Shah, after personal inquiry, ordered the release of the prisoner, and on being informed some days later that this had not been done, the Telegraph-master was directed to take the telegraphic royal command to the prison, and see it instantly obeyed. The official carried out his instructions, and the guards at once set the prisoner free.

The system of farming out the provinces gives rise to much grumbling, which perhaps, on close examination, may be found to be without full reason. The real cause of complaint is the absence of fair fixed taxation demands. Every village has to pay a tithe of its annual value to the State, and previous to collection the place is visited by one of the provincial officials, and the fullest details of the circumstances of each family are ascertained. The limit of the official robbery which follows is the ability to pay, as measured by the patience of the sufferers. The peasantry are peaceful, frugal, and easily governed, but there is a point beyond which they cannot be pressed without risk of making them turn on the oppressor. They have now learnt the strength of the defence they possess in the power of making their grievances known. No doubt the provincial levy of taxation charges doubles the State tithe, one-half of the whole amount being taken by the Governor and the officials; but all this does not mean more than one-fifth of the village income, for the general assessment was made before the existing improvement in the circumstances of the cultivators had taken place more or less all over the country. There was then little demand for products which are now exported and paid for in gold, thus giving a high price in the silver currency of the country. After the provincial taxation, there are local charges, which may possibly add a further 2 or 3 per cent, to the total amount. Formerly insecurity and want of confidence confined cultivation and stock-breeding to the barest limits, but it is evident now that the inhabitants can look to enjoy the fruits of their labour, and they are extending their fields of exertion. On the whole, it may be said that the peasantry and labouring classes in Persia are fairly well off, and I think their condition can bear a favourable comparison with that of the same classes in other countries.

In the course of my journeying in Persia, I generally found excellent quarters in the village houses. The rather mean outer appearance of the dwellings conveys the idea of poor accommodation within, but the reality is a pleasing disclosure of plain but well-carpeted rooms, with dados of matting or felt for the backs of the sitters by the wall. I always looked out for village lodgings when travelling off the main roads, and in wintry weather they were very comfortable from their open well-built clay fireplaces giving out heat without the nuisance of smoke. On these occasions I had ample opportunity to observe the every-day life of the people, and I was struck with much which showed that their manners and ways had been favourably touched and turned by a softening civilization of old date. I also there saw clear evidence of the origin of the Eastern shoe question, a matter which has often given rise to warm discussion in Persia and India; I allude to the removal of shoes on entering the inner rooms of a house. In India it is taken to imply inferiority, and since the establishment of British supremacy the custom has never been complied with by a European except in cases of personal employment in a native State. I remember an instance in point when a sergeant piper of a Highland regiment took service with one of the Punjab Sikh chiefs, to instruct a bagpipe band which the Rajah had formed in admiration of Scottish Highland music. In the contract paper which set forth in detail the duties, pay, and allowances of the instructor, the sergeant expressly stipulated that he should not be required to remove his shoes on entering the Rajah's room when a European was present. The origin of the custom of removing the shoes was clearly to avoid soiling the carpets in the house or tent, on which the inmates sat, ate, and slept.

Felts and rush-mats, no doubt, formed the first floor-coverings for tents and houses; but as arts and manufactures grew in Central Asia, the pastoral tribes, with whom, there being little or no agricultural work for the women and children, the woollen industries began, introduced carpets with coloured designs, many of the patterns of which are known to be of very old date, and still remain in the hands of certain families as their own carefully-guarded secrets and property. These carpets then became their pictures, framed in felt side-strips, on which people sat, slept, and transacted business. At meals the centre is covered with a cloth, on which the dishes are placed; and I think the carpet is regarded similarly as a well-polished dining-table was in the West in olden days, when the cloth was removed at the end of the courses. At other times it may be supposed that the pretty carpets are their pictures on the floor, just as ours are on the wall; in fact, many carpets of old design are so lovely and delicate that they are hung on the walls of European residents' houses in Persia as being too good to be trodden on. In the village houses the peasants always leave their shoes at the inner doors, and when a man arrives in riding-boots, with no intention of staying long, he complies with the object of the custom by sitting on the edge of the carpet, or felt, and tucking his legs underneath him, so that the feet may not touch or soil it. In this there is no question of inferior and superior, for all are socially equal; it is merely a matter of good manners and friendly feeling, just as signified in the West by removal of the hat or cap. It would appear that in the reception of Western Envoys at the Court of Persia it was customary to change the boots or shoes for slippers, or to cover them with these; but the practice was generally regarded as derogatory to the dignity of the national representative, and sometimes became the subject of strong protest and resentment. There is reason to believe that the custom always cropped up with every Envoy as an annoying cause of heated discussion and disagreeable feeling. On the occasion of the reception of Mr. Anthony Jenkinson, Queen Elizabeth's Envoy at the Court of Persia in 1561, this shoe question assumed an acute form; and when a pair of the Shah's slippers was sent to him to be worn at the interview with his Majesty, it is said that what was meant as attention was taken for insult. The interview took place without the slippers being used, and the meeting was not of a cordial character.

But besides this shoe difficulty at the Court of Persia, there was also a divergence of opinion regarding the lower garments, as the tight knee-breeches and hose of the West were considered improper in the East, and it is believed that the roomy Turkish *shalwar* trousers were required to be worn as 'overalls' to hide the legs on occasions of royal audience. In connection with this phase of Eastern idea, an incident happened with Sir Douglas Forsyth's diplomatic mission to the Amir of Kash-gar in 1873-74, which is worth mentioning here. The camp-sergeant with the mis-sion was Sergeant Rhind, of the 92nd Highlanders, and on the Envoy and staff being received at Yarkand by the Governor of that province, the second highest dignitary in the kingdom, it was understood that, as he was most exacting in the full obser-vance of all formalities, much would depend upon his report of our demeanour, appearance, and general conduct. This Governor kept quite a little Court, and we accordingly paid our visit in all the show of a dress parade. Sergeant Rhind attended in kilted uniform, and his appearance attracted considerable shy and sly notice. Ma-homed Yunis, the Governor, was a man of severe ideas, and while pretending not to see the Highlander, who stood behind us during the interview, he was reported to say after our departure that his costume appeared to be incomplete. Some weeks afterwards, on our reaching Kashgar, the capital in the North, and preparing for the formal audience of the Sovereign, the famous Ataligh Ghazi, the Court master of the ceremonies, appeared suddenly before the appointed time, and announced most peremptorily that the sergeant was to accompany us fully dressed. He explained that the kilt with bare knees was objectionable, and could not be tolerated at the Ataligh's Court; so the trews had to be substituted for the showy garb of old Gaul. The indoor dress worn by Persian ladies is not unlike our Highland kilt.

The shoe question was finally settled in a clause of the Turkmanchai treaty of 1828, which is accepted by all the foreign legations. It provides that goloshes or shoe-coverings shall be worn, to be removed before entering the audience-room or going into the Shah's presence, and this practice continues at the present time. The 'dragoman' establishments are much more attached to old ideas than Turks and Persians, and they cling to their presumed monopoly of knowledge of all Court and social customs in order to enhance their importance. The Persians move with the times, and understand Western modes of showing respect; yet I heard it said by a local light that it was a breach of good taste to salute the Shah by lifting the hat, and that it offended Mohammedan notions of propriety to remove the head-covering in society. Accordingly, I once saw some European gentlemen wearing their hats in the reception-room of one of the Shah's Ministers; but on observing others who were known to be well acquainted with Persian feeling entering with hat in hand, they, who were under the guidance of a 'dragoman', adopted the European custom.

In Fraser's 'Persia', we are told that when Shah Abbas the Great received Sir Dodmore Cotton, Ambassador from James I., his Majesty, 'being desirous of pleasing his guests, drank to the health of the King of England. At the name of his Sovereign the Ambassador stood up and took off his hat. Abbas smiled, and likewise raised his turban in token of respect.'

The farming system which is applied to the Customs in Persia continues to cause considerable loss to the State. An extension of the same direct control as is exercised in the Telegraph Department would show most favourable results. Under the present short-sighted system the interests of all the contractors lie in suppressing correct information and giving misleading statistics, so that the annual bidding may be kept low. But notwithstanding this, the truth leaks out to indicate that trade in Persia is increasing. There are now signs of practical advice at Tehran, to consider the establishment of a properly constituted Persian control Board of Customs, by which a well-organized service, under the central authority, may be maintained, and a considerable increase of revenue secured. It may be said that all merchants in Persia benefit by the farming system, for under it they can arrange to have their goods passed on payment of a lump sum, and with but the merest show of examination of invoices. In this manner they manage to get consignments through the Customs at less than the fixed tariff. On a late rumour of a foreign control of the Customs being likely, the Russian Armenian merchants engaged in trade in the North frankly represented the fact of arrangements being made with the authorities at the ports, to take less than the treaty 5 per cent. on exports and imports, and they urged that the custom was of such old date and long continuance as to make it a fully recognised right. They stated that their trade was established on this basis, and they protested against any change. There can be no doubt that the same custom prevails in the South, and all along the frontier. As the farming contracts are much subdivided, competition operates to reduce rates, so as to induce change of trade routes. Thus, I heard of a merchant in Central Persia, whose communications are with the South, asking a contractor in the North for a quotation of his terms, so as to make it advantageous for him to send his goods that way. In the matter of contraband articles, the farming system lends itself to encourage the passing of what the State forbids, as the middlemen and their servants are tempted to make as much money as possible during the short time of their annual contract engagements. In a country like Persia, where pride of arms prevails to keep up the habit of carrying them, there is a steady demand for modern breech-loading rifles. The Government is alive to the necessity of preventing the importation of firearms, and from time to time seizures are made of consignments smuggled under the guise of merchandise. With a large nomad and semi-nomad population of warlike and predatory instincts, almost every man of whom lays by money most diligently, bit by bit, for the purchase of a breechloader and cartridges, it is obvious that the interests of Government call for the strongest check to the foreign trade in arms; but it may be taken for granted that so long as the Customs are farmed out on the present system the supply will be passed in to meet the demand. The favourite weapon is the Martini-Henry, and there are many thousands in the possession of the nomads and villagers. This rifle, as the Peabody-Martini, was first introduced into the country during the late Turko-Russian War, when, being the Turkish army weapon, it fell by thousands into the hands of Russian soldiers, who sold them to the Persian sutlers and pedlars allowed to accompany the troops. The Persians had shown their usual energy and enterprise abroad by becoming camp-traders with the Russian forces engaged on active service in Asia Minor, and they sent the captured arms, which they purchased in large numbers, over the border into Persia, where they fetched good prices. A profitable trade in cartridges followed the introduction of the new rifle, and judging by the well-filled belts and bandoliers which I saw on the North-western frontier (Kurdistan and Azerbaijan), the business appears to be a well established one. In the course of time and trade this rifle found its way South to the fighting Bakhtiaris, Lurs, and Arabs, and the general vote in its favour brought about a supply of 'trade' Martini-Henry arms imported by way of the Persian Gulf, so that now in Persia what is known as the 'Marteen' has become the popular arm in private possession. The 'Remington' has its possessors and admirers among the Karun Arab tribes, who get their arms from Baghdad and Turkish sources. There is a brisk trade in ammunition for the breechloader, and so keen is the desire to secure and supplement the supply that solid-drawn brass cartridge-cases, which admit of being used over and over again, with boxes of caps and sets of reloading apparatus, are now in brisk demand.

At Kasvin our eyes were refreshed with the sight of the excellently-equipped Indo-European telegraph line, which comes in there from Tabriz and the North, and passes on to Tehran and India. This line, with its wires carried on tall iron standard posts stretching far in a dominating manner over the country, seems to stand forth as a strong witness to the effectual command and control exercised by the Shah's Government at the present time. On the first establishment of this line there was much conjecture as to the great risk of continued interruption from the mischief of man; and failure to complete the land working at the outset dissatisfied commercial men in England, so that to maintain certain communication the Red Sea cable was laid. But new land lines were erected which worked equally well as the cable, and the firm insistence by the Persian Government on heavy damages for all malicious injury gradually developed the perfect security which comes from local interests demanding the fullest protection. The service by this line is now as certain and quick as that of the ocean cable; in fact, I think the average speed of messages between London and Calcutta is greater *via* Tehran than *via* Suez. There was an interesting race last year between the companies to communicate to India the result of the Derby, and it was won in a way by the cable line. The messages were simultaneously despatched from Epsom, that by Tehran reaching Bombay five seconds before the other, but as the name of the winning horse only was given correctly, Karachi, six hundred miles distant, had to be asked for a repetition of the names of the second and third horses. The cable telegram gave the three names accurately. Had Karachi been agreed upon as the point of arrival for India, instead of Bombay, the Indo-European would have won this telegraph race.

CHAPTER III.

--Kasvin grapes --Persian wine --Vineyards in Persia --Wine manufacture --Mount Demavend --Afshar volcanic region --Quicksilver and gold --Tehran water-supply --Village quarrels --Vendetta --Tehran tramways --Bread riots --Mint and copper coin.

The grape harvest was being gathered at Kasvin as we passed through. The place is well known for its extensive vineyards and fine fruit-gardens. Its golden grapes have a wide reputation, and these, with the white species, also grown there, are in steady demand for wine manufacture, which is carried on in the town, notwithstanding the greatly disproportionate number of Moullas among the inhabitants. Large quantities of the grapes are also sent to Tehran for wine purposes there. Persia keeps up the character for strong wine which it had 600 B.C., when the Scythian invaders took to it so eagerly as to establish the saying, 'As drunk as a Scythian.' It was said that these hard-headed, deep-drinking, wild warriors were always thirsting for 'another skinful,' and were ever ready to declare that the last was always the best. Eighteen hundred years later, Hafiz, the merry poet, sang aloud the praises of Shiraz wine, which to this day bears a high reputation in Persia, a reputation which was royally good in the traditional bygone time long before Cyrus, when it appears to have been highly appreciated in the festivities of Glorious Jamshed, the founder of Persepolis. The poet Omar Khayyam, in moralizing over the ruins of the fallen splendour of that famous place, speaks in Fitzgerald's 'Rubaiyat':

'They say the lion and the lizard keep
  The Court where Jamshed gloried and drank deep.'

The Persian poet-historian Firdausi ascribes to Jamshed the discovery of wine in his leisure from kingly duties and scientific pursuits, for to him is attributed the invention of many useful arts, and the introduction of the solar year for measurement of time, the first day of which, when the sun enters Aries, he ordered to be celebrated by a splendid festival. It is called Nauroz, or New Year's Day, and is still the greatest festival in Persia. This single institution of former days, under a different religion and system of measuring time, has triumphed over the introduction of Mohammedanism, and is observed with as much joy and festivity now as it was by the ancient inhabitants of Persia.

According to Moulla Akbar's manuscripts, quoted in Malcolm's 'History of Persia,' Jamshed was immoderately fond of grapes, and desired to preserve some which were placed in a large vessel and lodged in a vault for future use. When the vessel was opened, the grapes had fermented, and their juice in this state was so acid that the King believed it must be poisonous. He had some other vessels filled with the juice, and 'Poison' written upon each; these were placed in his room. It happened that one of his favourite ladies was afflicted with nervous headaches, the pain of which distracted her so much that she desired death, and observing a vessel with 'Poison' written on it, she took it and swallowed its contents. The wine, for such it had become, overpowered the lady, who fell down in a sound sleep, and awoke much refreshed. Delighted with the remedy, she repeated the doses so often that the King's 'poison' was all drunk. He soon discovered this, and forced the lady to confess what she had done. A quantity of wine was then made, and Jamshed and all his Court drank of the new beverage, which, from the circumstance that led to its discovery, is to this day known in Persia as *zahr-i-khush*, or the pleasing poison. After that the manufacture of wine became a regular industry, and spread from Shiraz, where it originated. At the present time the process of manufacture is similar to what it was then, in that the grape-juice is collected in large Ali-Baba-like jars and buried in the ground. Alexander the Great is said to have followed the festive example of his royal predecessor, and to have drunk deep in the majestic halls of Persepolis. It has been supposed by some that he caused the splendid palaces there to be set on fire in a drunken freak.

As a pendant to the story of a lady's discovery, in the time of Jamshed, of wine as an efficacious cure for nervous headache, another is told which ascribes to a lady the withdrawal of a royal decree against the sale and use of wine. The Shah Hussein, on his accession to the throne in 1694, displayed his religious zeal by forbidding the sale of wine, and he ordered the destruction of all the stock of it that was in the royal cellars at Ispahan. But his grandmother, by feigning herself ill, and wholly dependent upon wine for cure, not only prevailed upon him to revoke the decree, but also persuaded him to drink some in pure regard to herself, with the result that he fell away from priestly influence and became a tippler. Unfortunately for the nation, this grandmother's guidance led Shah Hussein to ruin by wine and women, and dragged him down to the deep degradation of surrendering Persia to the cruel tyranny of the Afghan occupation.

Wood being scarce in Persia, and poles, stakes, and sticks for upright and lateral support not being easily procurable, the mode of culture of the vine has come to be by planting in deep broad trenches, with high sloping banks, up and over which the stems and branches run and fall. The trenches are made to lie so as to allow of the bank-slopes having the best exposure. This is the system followed on the flat, but in hilly ground, by means of careful trimming and the assistance of piled stones, the plants are made to develop strong standard stems, with bunchy, bushy tops. I was particularly struck a few years ago with the neat, well-tended vineyards at the village of Imam-Zadeh-Ismail, in the hills about forty miles north-west of Persepolis. Almost the whole of the village lands were laid out in vineyards, well walled and beautifully kept. The vines looked as if they were tended by those who understood their culture well, and they appeared to thrive wonderfully on the light soil of the place. Surprising energy had been shown in clearing the ground, which was naturally stony; and there was abundant evidence of much patient labour in the garden-like enclosures. Vineyards occupied all the flat ground on which the village stood, and they extended up the slopes. Hillside clearing was going on all around for further planting of vines, which were seen to flourish there. Raisins are largely made there, and I was told by my Kashkai conductor (for I was well off the beaten track and required a guide), who seemed to know what he was talking about, that the fresh grapes were used for wine, but not in the village. The religious character of the chief inhabitants of the village, who are sheikhs, and guardians of the Holy Shrine of the mausoleum of the Imam-Zadeh-Ismail, which lies within its limits, prevents the preparation there of the forbidden fermented juice of the grape. The shrine is endowed with the village lands rent free, and all these lands are devoted to vine cultivation. The vineyards at Shiraz have been greatly extended of late years, and particular attention is now paid to the cultivation of the Kholar grape, as the best suited for wine. This grape takes its name from the village of Kholar, which is within a few miles of the town. Tabriz, Hamadan, Isfahan, and Shiraz produce the best wine in Persia. Red and white are made at all these places; the white wine of Hamadan is a sort of strong sauterne, and some of it has quite a delicate flavour; Isfahan produces a wine of a port character, and the best shiraz is sometimes like new madeira. All these wines resemble in strength those that are now made in Australia. Something is wanting in the mode of manufacture to make the wine capable of improvement with keeping, and also of bearing transport. The advent of the Russian road will probably lead to the development of Kasvin's large area of fruitful vines, and the success which has attended vineyard industry at Derbend, on the Caspian, may encourage similar enterprise there.

As neither law nor custom forbids the manufacture of wine by non-Mohammedans, the cultivation of the grape spreads, and the making of wine increases. From this it may be inferred, as there is little export of wine from Persia, that all the produce is not consumed by non-Mohammedans. As a matter of fact, the religious law which forbids wine to Mohammedans is not rigidly observed; in truth, they are not all total abstainers, and the delightful poison, as chronicled by Moulla Akbar, is known to be a convenient remedy for all manner of moods, ills, and complaints, nervous, imaginary, and real. They have been described as drinking well when they do break the religious law, for they have a saying that 'there is as much sin in a glass as in a flagon.' The Persians have never thoroughly accommodated themselves to the creed of their Semitic conquerors; they show profound respect for the externals of Mohammedanism, and are sincere in their practice of piety and the obligations of religion and charity; but they have always indulged in the fancies and ideas of the great school of free-thinking philosopher Sofis, whose observance of the ordinances of severe and joyless life is notedly lax.

The weather was lovely as we journeyed over the Kasvin plain to Tehran, towards the end of September. Autumn in the North of Persia is a gloriously fine season, almost spring-like in many ways, and, indeed, it is called there the 'second spring.' The landscape then, though nearly barren of verdure, has a beauty of its own in warm soft colours, and the atmospheric effects on the hills and distances, evening and morning, are of wonderfully delicate tones and tints. The prominent feature in the landscape near Tehran is the grand cone-shaped Mount Demavend, about forty miles to the north-east, which shoots up 19,400 feet above ocean-level, and overtops all the surrounding heights by 6,000 feet or more. It stood out bold, cold, and clear against the blue sky, and looked beautifully white with a fresh covering of new snow, and it was more than usually distinct, from being clear of the cloud-crown it usually wears. In the evening the massive peak presented a splendid appearance, looking as in a white heat from the shine of the setting sun, which, though lost to view below the horizon, yet lighted up the old volcano.

Demavend has long been asleep, but the great earthquakes of 1891, 1893 and 1895 in Astrabad and Kuchan to the eastward, and Khalkhal in the north-west, show that its underground fires are still alight. The scene of the last is about one hundred miles north-east of the old volcanic region of Afshar, remarkable for its remains of vast 'cinter' cones, formed by the flowing geysers of long, long ago, and which were shattered and scattered by some mighty explosion, when the great geysers boiled up and burst their walls. Here is seen the Takht-i-Suliman, a ruined fort of very ancient date, which local tradition describes as one of King Solomon's royal residences, shared by his Queen, Belgheiz (of Sheba), whose summer throne is also shown on a mountain height above. This ruin incloses a flowing geyser of tepid sea-green water, about 170 feet deep, the temperature of which was 66 deg. when I visited the place in 1892. Near it is the Zindan-i-Suliman (Solomon's Dungeon), an extinct geyser, 350 feet deep. It shows as a massive 'cinter' cone, 440 feet high, standing prominently up in the plain. This district was visited and fully described by the late Sir Henry Rawlinson, and a further account of it has been given by Mr. Theodore Bent, who, with Mrs. Bent, went there in 1889.

The volcanic district of Afshar has long been known for its quicksilver, which from time to time has been found in small quantities. Some seven or eight hundred years ago Arab miners laboured long in their search for the main cinnabar vein which undoubtedly lies hidden there, and their wide workings in laying open a whole hillside, where signs of cinnabar are still seen, show what great gangs of labourers they must have had at their command. The Persian Mines Corporation in 1891-92 engaged in operations at the same point, but, after considerable sinking of shafts and driving of galleries into the heart of the hill, they decided to cease work, being disappointed, like their Arab predecessors, in not finding quickly what they had traced by clear signs up to its mountain source. A few miles below the site of these cinnabar-mine operations there are ancient gold-washing workings, and within thirty miles are heavy veins of quartz.

Tehran displays a marked advance in many of the resources of civilization; houses of an improved style are springing up, the roadways are better attended to, and there is a great increase in the number of carriages. The Prime Minister's new house, near the British Legation, is situated in beautiful gardens, set off with pretty lakelets and terraced grounds, which give slopes for flowing waterfalls. These gardens, in common with all in the town, are tenanted every year by nightingales of sweet song. It is now proposed to enclose an adjoining available space to form a people's park, which would be a great place of enjoyment in summer to a people of poetic imagination like the Persians, who delight in the green glade with the cool sound of flowing water. The severe cholera epidemic of 1892 showed the absolute necessity of an improvement in the rude sanitary system which then existed, and a beginning has been made in the daily careful cleaning of the streets and removal of refuse. But a better and increased water-supply is greatly needed for the town, which is becoming larger every year. People who have money to spend appear to be attracted more than ever to the capital. Those who before were content with the provincial towns now build houses in Tehran. The superior houses have garden-ground attached, and much tree-planting is done. The demand for water increases, but the supply is not supplemented. Years ago the utmost was made of the sources from which water is drawn; no pains have been spared to extract every possible drop of water from the heart of the hills within a considerable distance, and to convey it undiminished by evaporation to the city. This is done by underground channels called ***kanats***, which are excavated with great ingenuity and skill, and are marvels of industry. This system prevails all over Persia, and existence as well as the fertility of the soil mainly depends on the water-supply thus obtained. The sandy expanse round Yezd in the desert of South-eastern Persia has been made literally to blossom like the rose by means of these subterranean channels, some of which are tunnelled for a distance of thirty miles. I was there in spring-time, and was then able to see what a wonder-worker water is in Persia.

The pressing need of more water for Tehran has now drawn attention to the proposals of some years ago for increasing the supply. One of these was to divert to the south an affluent of the Upper Lar, which rises in the Elburz range, and flows into the Caspian. It was seen that this could be done by cutting a new channel and tunnelling from a point sufficiently high, where the stream runs in an elevated valley between the double ridge of the range. The work would have been similar, but simpler, to what was completed last year in Madras, where the upper Periyar stream was changed from a western to an eastern flow. The execution of the Lar project would be easy, and it would not practically affect the volume of water in the main stream, which receives many tributaries below the proposed point of piercing the watershed. But the Lar Valley was one of the Shah's summer retreats, and a favourite pasture-ground for his brood mares and young stock. It is, moreover, a popular resort of flock-owning nomads, and as the Shah's love of camp life there led him to fear injury to the grassy plains and slopes of his favourite highlands, the project was abandoned.

There was another scheme to construct a series of reservoirs by means of strong barriers at the foot of the lower ravines of the Elburz range, eight miles north of Tehran, in which to keep the winter water which comes from the melting snow. The whole mountain-chain is covered with snow each year from top to bottom. In April and May the snow melts, and the precious water flows away where it is not wanted. Were this water stored, it would be made available in the succeeding hot months. The sloping plain between the hills and the town is capable, with irrigation, of great fertility, and the construction of these reservoirs would prove a veritable gold-mine.

The distribution of water is a most important part of village administration in Persia. The work of cutting off and letting on water with most exact observance of time-measurements is carried out by a waterman called *mirab* (lord of the water) whose office is hereditary, subject, however, to the special judgment of popular opinion. The duties demand a clear head and nimble foot, and the waterman, in hastening from point to point, has to show all the alertness of a street lamplighter. He has to keep a correct count of time, for water is apportioned by the hour, and his memory for all the details of change, sale, and transfer must be good and unchallenged. When he becomes too old, or otherwise incapacitated for the performance of his work with the necessary quickness, he avails himself of the assistance of a son or someone whom he proposes with the village approval to bring up as his successor. The old man is then to be seen going leisurely along the water-courses which issue from the underground channels, accompanied by his young deputy carrying the long-handled Persian spade, ready to run and execute his orders. Disputes between village and village over **kanat** water-cuts form the subject of severe fights occasionally, and the saying is that water and women are the main causes of village quarrels in Persia.

It was a hot day in June, and having been up before daylight so as to start at earliest dawn and avoid the mid-day heat for my whole party, we were all in the enjoyment of afternoon sleep, when the courtyard was invaded by a shouting mob of excited villagers, calling on me to hear their story and bear witness to their wounds. They said they were the tenants of the landlord whose house I was occupying, and they begged me as his guest to make a statement of their case, so that justice might be done. There had been a dispute over an irrigation channel, and the opposing side having mustered strong, they were overpowered by numbers and badly beaten. Some of the hurts they had received were ugly to look at, having been inflicted with the long-handled Persian spade, the foot-flanges of which make it a dangerous weapon. After a patient hearing, and getting some plaster and simple dressing for their cuts and bruises, they went away satisfied. So much for water as a cause of quarrel, but an instance of the other cause, woman, which had come under my notice shortly before, was more seriously characteristic. It occurred at Shamsabad, on the border of the Aberkoh Desert, between Yezd and Shiraz. I halted there after the long night journey across the desert, and immediately I was settled in my village quarters, the master of the house in which I lodged asked me to look at the gunshot wounds of one of his young men, and to prescribe and provide in any way I could towards healing them. I asked if any bones were broken, saying that I could do little or nothing in such a case. I was told that they were but flesh wounds, and on the young man coming in, I was shown a ragged long cut between the lower ribs, and a deepish wound in the fleshy part of the leg, which had evidently been made by slugs or buckshot. I prescribed careful cleansing, and the use of lint and lotion, and I gave a supply of the necessary material. I asked how the thing had happened, and the young fellow told me that he and his brother had been treacherously attacked at a water-mill, whilst having the family grain ground, by some Aberkoh youths, between whose family and his there was a longstanding blood-feud; that they both had been shot at close quarters, and his brother had died of his wounds two days before.

The master of the house, who was also headman of the village, explained that the blood-feud had been carried on for five generations, and had originated in a 'little maid' who, being betrothed in their village, had eloped with a young man of Aberkoh. The disappointed bridegroom had afterwards taken his successful rival's life, and the deadly demand of a life for a life had, in accordance with the law of revenge, been made and exacted for the past five generations. He said the elders had hoped the quarrel was nearly dead, as there had been long peace between the parties, but suddenly the hot blood of youth had risen to renew it, and now there was fear of further murder. In that remote district the ancient first principles of natural justice had still strong hold upon the people, and formed, in the absence of established law, the defence of families and communities.

The knowledge that a man is considered disgraced who allows the blood of his father or brother to pass unrevenged makes many a murderer in thought pause, and depart from the deed. Accordingly, in those lawless parts, as a rule, order reigns, and disputes and differences are discussed by the village 'gray-beards,' who generally are able to arrange a compromise. But in the reckless rage of a lost love the deed is done, which carries its fatal consequences to future generations, as in the case I have mentioned. I told the old village headman, who was really the local judge, that in some of the wild parts of Firanghistan there were similar occurrences, and that the best form of reconciliation in the present instance would be 'wife for wife,' the first offending family giving a girl-love to a husband-lover on the other side, and thus finally closing the quarrel in the happiest manner. I said that under such circumstances intermarriages were generally the best means of improving friendship and terminating feuds between families.

The Tehran street tramways continue to work, though the profit return is small. The company began with graduated fares, but I heard they were considering a minimum general charge, which it was thought would encourage more traffic, especially in the visits of women to one another, as their outdoor dress is unsuited to walking in comfort. The tramway cars have separate compartments for women.

The travelling pace is necessarily slow, in order to avoid hurt or harm to people and animals in the crowded thoroughfares. In the East, accidents at the hands of Europeans or their employes are not readily understood or easily accepted as such. The Tehran Tramways Company has had its trials in this respect. At one time it was the heavy hurt of a boy, son of a Syud, one of the 'pure lineage', a descendant of the family of the Prophet, on which the populace, roused by the lashing lamentations of the father, damaged the car and tore up the line. On another occasion a man, in obstinate disregard of warning, tried to enter at the front, and was thrown under the wheels. Again the excitable bystanders were worked up to fury and violence, and the Governor of the town gave judgment against the company for 'blood-money'. The counter-claim for damage done to the line enabled a compromise to be effected. Oriental indifference is the chief cause of the accidents. 'It is impossible but that offences will come, but woe unto him through whom they come.' For 'offences', the Oriental reading is 'accidents'.

In all large Persian towns there is a numerous class of 'roughs' known as the ***kullah-numdah*** (felt-caps; they wear a brown hard-felt low hat without a brim), excitable and reckless, and always ready for disturbance. They are the 'casuals', who live from hand to mouth, those to whom an appeal can be made by the careful working class when the price of bread is run up to famine figure, owing to the 'cornering' of wheat, which of late years has been much practised in Persia. The baker used to be the first victim of popular fury in a bread riot, and it is said that one was baked alive in his own oven. But in these times of grain speculation in Persia, the people have learnt to look in 'wheat corners' for the real cause of dear bread, and in consequence the bread riots have become more formidable, as was proved lately at Tabriz. On a previous occasion the Vali Ahd (now H.I.M. the Shah), who, as Governor-General of Azerbaijan, resided at Tabriz, found himself unable to cope with the difficulty, and abandoned his projected visit to Tehran, so as to apply the money he had provided for it to cheapening bread for the people. This practical pocket-sympathy with them secured a popularity which will bring its reward.

Next to the 'wheat-ring' as a cause of disturbance and riot comes what may be called the 'copper-ring' of Tehran, which is likely to produce serious trouble throughout the country. The Royal Mint in Persia is worked on the farming system, the evils of which have now extended to the currency. The low price of copper allows of it being coined at an enormous profit, and advantage has been taken of this to a dangerous extent. The whole country is now poisoned with 'black money,' as the coppers are called, and it is at a heavy discount. This bears cruelly on the labouring classes and all who are paid in copper coin. Owing to exchange with Europe keeping above silver, that metal cannot be imported and coined, so as to give a gain to the Mint-master, who has no idea of sacrificing any of the great profit he has made on copper. No silver has been coined since March, 1895, and this is the Mint-master's excuse for sending out copper in great quantities, to take the place of silver. Twenty copper shahi go to a kran (present exchange value 4-1/2d.), and in the absence of silver employers of labour pay wholly in copper, which for bazaar purposes is at a discount, so much so that, when a purchase is beyond question above a kran in amount, an agreement as to payment in silver or copper is first made, and then the bargaining begins. In a country where money bears a high value, as proved by the fact that accounts are still reckoned in dinars, an imaginary coin, of which one thousand go to a silver kran and fifty to a copper shahi, the depreciation I have mentioned is a very serious affair, for it touches the mass of the people sorely. When travelling off the beaten track in Persia, I have always been amused and interested in hearing my head-servant announce loudly in a tone of importance and satisfaction to my village host for the night that I had ordered so many 'thousands' to be given for house-room, fuel, barley, straw, etc. The kran was never mentioned; it was always a 'thousand.'[1]

1 Since the above was written, information has been received that the late Shah, about three weeks before his death, promulgated a decree directing the Mint coinage of copper to be suspended for a term of five years, and intimating that the Customs, Post-office and Telegraph departments would accept copper coin to a certain amount in cash transactions, at a fixed rate. And, further, arrangements have been made with the Imperial Bank of Persia to purchase, on account of the Government, copper coin up to a certain sum, from small *bona-fide* holders who are in possession of it in the regular course of retail business for the necessaries of life.

CHAPTER IV.

The late Shah was always liberal and conciliatory in the treatment of his Christian subjects throughout the country, and this is a matter which, at the present time, deserves special notice. In the history of Persia many proofs of friendly feeling towards Christians are to be found, and the sovereigns appear to have led the popular mind in the way of goodwill to them. Shah Abbas the Great was an example of kind and considerate tolerance, and it was Shah Abbas II who said of them, 'It is for God, not for me to judge of men's consciences: and I will never interfere with what belongs to the tribunal of the Great Creator and Lord of the universe.' The Western Christian missionaries are fully protected in their mission work among the Eastern Christians in Persia on the understanding that they do not actively and directly engage in proselytizing Mohammedans.

The American Presbyterian is the only mission in Tehran, and it carries on its work so smoothly and judiciously that the sensitive susceptibilities of the most fanatical Moullas are never roused nor ruffled. They have succeeded well by never attempting too much. They show their desire to benefit all classes and creeds, and during the severe cholera outbreak In 1892 the hospital they established in the city for the medical treatment of all comers up to the utmost extent of their accommodation and ability was a powerful and convincing proof of their good work and will. The disease was of a very fatal type, and its deadly ravages called forth a display of devotion and self-sacrifice which deserved and obtained the highest commendation from all Persians and Europeans.

While on this subject, the splendid example set by the Governor of the town, the Vazir Isa Khan, should be noticed. He was very wealthy, and did much to relieve the sufferings and wants of the poor who were attacked by the disease. He remained in the city while the epidemic raged, and would not seek safety in flight to the adjoining mountains, as many had done. But, sad to say, he fell a victim at the last, and his wife, who had remained with him throughout, died of the disease two days before him.

It will be remembered that in 1891 an agitation was raised regarding the reported abduction of an Armenian girl, named Katie Greenfield, by a Kurd in Persian Kurdistan. An attempt which was made to take the girl back to her family caused the couple to cross the frontier into Turkish Kurdistan, and great excitement among the Kurds on both sides of the border was created. The contention grew, and commissioners and consuls, with troops, Persian and Turkish, took part in it. In the end it was made perfectly clear that the girl had gone off with Aziz, the Kurd, as the husband of her own choice, and had embraced the Mohammedan faith by her own wish. The Kurds in Persian Kurdistan appear to live on friendly terms with their Armenian village neighbours, and on this occasion a runaway love-match became the cause of some popular excitement in England, and much trouble and tumult on the Perso-Turkish frontier.

The Armenian Archbishop in Persia, who resides at Isfahan, is always a Russian subject from the monastery of Etchmiadzin, near Erivan, the seat of the Catholicus, the primate of the orthodox Armenian Church, and this doubtless has its effect in suggesting protection and security. France also for a longtime past has steadily asserted the right to protect the Catholic Armenian Church in Persia, and once a year the French Minister at Tehran, with the Legation secretaries, attends Divine service in the chapel there in full diplomatic dress and state, to show the fact and force of the support which the Church enjoys. France similarly takes Catholic institutions in Turkey under her protection, and appears to be generally the Catholic champion in the East.

The careful observer in Tehran cannot fail to be struck with the religious tolerance shown to non-Mohammedan Persian subjects in the 'shadow of the Shah.'

Amongst these, other than Christians, may be mentioned the Guebres (Parsees) and the Jews. Persecuted in the provinces, they receive liberal treatment in Tehran, and it is to be hoped that the late Shah's gracious example will in time be followed by his Majesty's provincial governors.

The Babi sect of Mohammedans, regarded as seceders from Islam, but who assert their claim to be only the advocates for Mohammedan Church reform, are at last better understood and more leniently treated--certainly at Tehran. They have long been persecuted and punished in the cruellest fashion, even to torture and death, under the belief that they were a dangerous body which aimed at the subversion of the State as well as the Church. But better counsels now prevail, to show that the time has come to cease from persecuting these sectarians, who, at all events in the present day, show no hostility to the Government; and the Government has probably discovered the truth of the Babi saying, that one martyr makes many proselytes.

The Babis aim at attracting to their ranks the intelligent and the learned, in preference to the ignorant and unlearned; and it is believed that now sufficient education whereby to read and write is absolutely necessary for membership. They wish to convince by example, and not by force, and this accounts for the absence of active resistance to the persecutions from which they often suffer most grievously. They say that they desire to return to original Mohammedanism, as it first came from the Arabian desert, pure and simple, and free from the harsh intolerance and arrogance which killed the liberal spirit in which it was conceived. They deplore the evil passions and fierce animosities engendered by religious differences; they tolerate all creeds having a common end for good, and seek to soften the hearts of those who persecute them, by showing that they but wish for peace on earth and goodwill to all men. They have a widespread organization throughout Persia, and many learned Moullas and Syuds have secretly joined them. They have always been firm in their faith, even unto death, rejecting the offer of life in return for a declaration against the Bab, him whom they regard as the messenger of good tidings.

An acknowledged authority on the Bab, the founder of this creed, has written that he 'directed the thoughts and hopes of his disciples to this world, not to an unseen world.' From this it was inferred he did not believe in a future state, nor in anything beyond this life. Of course, among the followers of a new faith, liberal and broad in its views, continued fresh developments of belief must be expected; and with reference to the idea that the Babis think not of a hereafter, I was told that they believe in the re-incarnation of the soul, the good after death returning to life and happiness, the bad to unhappiness. A Babi, in speaking of individual pre-existence, said to me, 'You believe in a future state; why, then, should you not believe in a pre-existent state? Eternity is without beginning and without end,' This idea of re-incarnation, generally affecting all Babis, is, of course, an extension of the original belief regarding the re-incarnation of the Bab, and the eighteen disciple-prophets who compose the sacred college of the sect.

Some time ago signs began to appear of a general feeling that the persecution of the Babis must cease. Many in high places see this, and probably say it, and their sympathy becomes known. At one time a high Mohammedan Church dignitary speaks regarding tolerance and progress in a manner which seems to mean that he sees no great harm in the new sect. Then a soldier, high in power and trust, refers to the massacres of Babis in 1890 and 1891 as not only cruel acts, but as acts of insane folly, 'for,' he said, 'to kill a Babi is like cutting down a chenar-tree, from the root of which many stems spring up, and one becomes many.' Then a Moulla, speaking of the necessity of a more humane treatment of the Babis, and others of adverse creeds, says that he looks for the time when all conditions of men will be equally treated, and all creeds and classes be alike before the law. Omar Khayyam, the astronomer-poet of Persia, who wrote about eight hundred years ago, gave open expression to the same liberal-minded views, urging tolerance and freedom for all religious creeds and classes.

The last murderous mob attack led by Moullas against the Babis occurred at Yezd in April, 1891. It was probably an outcome of the Babi massacre which had taken place at Isfahan the previous year, and which, owing to the fiercely hostile attitude of the priests, was allowed to pass unnoticed by any strong public condemnation. On that occasion a party of the sect, pursued by an excited and blood-thirsty mob, claimed the 'sanctuary' of foreign protection in the office of the Indo-European Telegraph Company, and found asylum there. Negotiations were opened with the Governor of the town, who arranged for a safe conduct to their homes under military escort. Trusting to this, the refugees quitted the telegraph-office, but had not proceeded far before they were beset by a furious crowd, and as the escort offered no effectual resistance, the unfortunates were murdered in an atrociously cruel manner. The Shah's anger was great on hearing of this shameful treachery, but as the Governor pleaded powerlessness from want of troops, and helplessness before the fanaticism of the frenzied mob led by Moullas, the matter was allowed to drop.

Considering the great numbers of Babis all over Persia, and the ease with which membership can be proved, it strikes many observers as strange that murderous outbreaks against them are not more frequent. The explanation is that, besides the accepted Babis, there is a vast number of close sympathizers, between whom and the declared members of the sect there is but one step, and a continued strong persecution would drive them into the ranks of the oppressed. It might then be found that the majority was with the Babis, and this fear is a fact which, irrespective of other arguments, enables the influential and liberal-minded Moullas to control their headstrong and over-zealous brethren.

The isolated outbreaks that do occur are generally produced by personal animosity and greed of gain. Just as has been known in other countries where a proscribed religion was practised in secret, and protection against persecution and informers secured by means of money, so in many places the Babis have made friends in this manner out of enemies. Individuals sometimes are troubled by the needy and unscrupulous who affect an excess of religious zeal, but these desist on their terms being met. Occasionally in a settlement of bazaar trading-accounts, the debtor, who is a Mohammedan, being pressed by his creditor, whom he knows to be a Babi, threatens to denounce him publicly in order to avoid payment.

I witnessed an instance of 'sanctuary' asylum being claimed in the stable of one of the foreign legations at Tehran by a well-known Persian merchant, a Babi, who fled for his life before the bazaar ruffians to whom his debtor had denounced him, urging them to smite and slay the heretic. It was believed that the practice of blackmailing the Babis was such a well-known successful one at Yezd that some of the low Mohammedans of the town tried to share in the profits and were disappointed. This, it was said, led to the massacre which occurred there in April, 1891.

The Babis, notwithstanding divergence of opinion on many points, yet attend the mosques and the Moulla teachings, and comply with all the outward forms of religion, in order to avert the anger which continued absence from the congregation would draw upon them from hostile and bigoted neighbours. Two of them were suddenly taxed in the Musjid with holding heterodox opinions, and were then accused of being Babis. The discussion was carried outside and into the bazaar, the accusers loudly reviling and threatening them. They were poor, and were thus unable to find protectors at once. When being pressed hard by an excited mob which had collected on the scene, an over-zealous friend came to their aid, and said, 'Well, if they are Babis, what harm have they done to anyone?'

On this the tumult began, and the ferocity of the fanatical crowd rose to blood-heat. The sympathizer was seized, and as the gathering grew, the opportunity to gratify private animosity and satisfy opposing interests was taken advantage of, and three other Babis were added, making six in all who were dragged before the Governor to be condemned as members of an accursed sect. The Moullas urged them to save their lives by cursing the Bab, but they all refused. The wives and children of some of them were sent for so that their feelings might be worked upon to renounce their creed and live, but this had no effect in shaking their resolution. When told that death awaited them, they replied that they would soon live again. When argued with on this point of their belief, they merely said that they could not say how it was to be, but they knew it would be so. They were then given over to the cruel mob, and were hacked to death, firm in their faith to the last.

The temptation to make away with others in a similar manner produced two more victims during the night, but these the Governor tried to save by keeping them in custody. The brutal mob, however, howled for their blood, and made such an uproar that the weak Governor, a youth of eighteen, surrendered them to a cruel death, as he had done the others. These two, like their brethren, refused to curse the Bab and live.

The Moullas have ever been defeated in their efforts to produce recantation from a Babi, and it is this remarkable steadfastness in their faith which has carried conviction into the hearts of many that the sect is bound to triumph in the end. The thoughtful say admiringly of them, as the Romans said of the Christians, whom they in vain doomed to death under every form of terror, 'What manner of men are these, who face a dreadful death fearlessly to hold fast to their faith?' An instance is mentioned of a Babi who did recant in order to escape the martyr's death, but he afterwards returned to his faith, and suffered calmly the death he had feared before.

The Moullas who led the Yezd massacre desired to associate the whole town in the crime, and called for the illumination of the bazaars in token of public joy. The order for this was given, but the Governor was warned in time to issue a countermand. It was found by the state of public feeling, and told to those in authority, who were able to realize the danger, that, as one-half or more of the shopkeepers were Babis, they would not have illuminated, for to have done so would imply approval of the murders and denial of their faith. Their determination to refuse to join in the demonstration of joy would have roused further mob fury, and the whole body of Babis, impelled by the instinct of self-preservation, would have risen to defend themselves.

The late Shah was deeply troubled and pained on hearing of this cruel massacre, and removed the Governor, who was his own grandson (being the eldest son of his Royal Highness the Zil-es-Sultan), notwithstanding the excuses urged in his favour, that the priestly power which roused the mob was too strong for him to act and prevent the murders. It is probable that the Government is assured of the peaceful nature of the Babi movement as it now exists; and with the orders to put an end to persecution, supported in some degree by popular feeling, we may hope to hear no more of such crimes as were committed at Isfahan and Yezd in 1890 and 1891.

The Babi reform manifests an important advance upon all previous modern Oriental systems in its treatment of woman. Polygamy and concubinage are forbidden, the use of the veil is discouraged, and the equality of the sexes is so thoroughly recognised that one, at least, of the nineteen sovereign prophets must always be a female. This is a return to the position of woman in early Persia, of which Malcolm speaks when he says that Quintus Curtius told of Alexander not seating himself in the presence of Sisygambis till told to do so by that matron, because it was not the custom in Persia for sons to sit in presence of their mother. This anecdote is quoted to show the great respect in which the female sex were held in Persia at the time of Alexander's invasion, and which also was regarded as one of the principal causes of the progress the country had made in civilization. The Parsees to this day conduct themselves on somewhat similar lines, and though we have not the opportunities of judging of maternal respect which were allowed to the Greeks, yet the fact of the same custom being shown in a father's presence at the present time seems to point to the rule of good manners to mothers being yet observed. And we know, from what happened on the death of Mohamed Shah in 1848, that a capable woman is allowed by public opinion to exercise openly a powerful influence in affairs of State at a critical time when wise counsels are required. The Queen-mother at that time became the president of the State Council, and cleverly succeeded in conciliating adverse parties and strengthening the Government, till the position of the young Shah, the late Sovereign, was made secure.

For a long time Russia and England were regarded as the only great Powers really interested in the future of Persia; but within the last few years it has been observed that Turkey, in showing an intention to consolidate her power in the Baghdad and Erzeroum pashaliks, was likely to be in a position to renew old claims on the Persian border. France has also lately increased her interest in Persia, and Germany has now entered the field of enterprise there in the practical manner of improving the road from Khani Kin, on the Turkish frontier, to Tehran, connecting it with a road from Baghdad. It will probably be found that this road-scheme belongs to the company under German auspices who are now constructing a railway which is ultimately to connect Baghdad with the Bosphorus, and part of which is already working. The trunk-line passes by Angora, Kaisarieh, Diarbekr, Mardin, and Mosul; and a loop-line leaves it at Eski Shehr, which, going by Konia, Marasch, and Orfa, rejoins it at Diarbekr.

There was an idea that, as Konia is a most promising field for the production of exports, the Smyrna lines competed so eagerly for the concession to extend there that the Porte was enabled to make terms with the Anatolian Railway Company (to which I have alluded) for the extension to Baghdad, which strategically is of great importance. It was said that the strong competition placed the Government in the position of the man in the Eastern story who went to the bazaar to sell an old camel, and a young cat of rare beauty. The cat was shown off sitting on the camel, and was desired by many purchasers; but there was no bid for the camel. The competition for the cat ran high, and then the owner announced that the one could not be sold without the other, on which the camel was bought with the cat. But as a matter of fact there was no opening for competition for the Konia branch. The Anatolian Railway had preferential rights for what is called the southern or loop line, which I have mentioned as passing through Konia, and rejoining the main or northern line at Diarbekr. They also have preferential rights of extension to Baghdad, and they mean to carry the line there.

The Smyrna Aidin railway has lately had a considerable improvement in its traffic, from the barley of Asia Minor being in increased demand in addition to its wheat. This means that the material for the beer as well as the bread of the masses elsewhere is found to be abundant and cheap there, and the extension of railway communication in those regions will most probably increase the supply and demand. The same trade in barley has lately sprung up in Southern Persia and Turkish Arabia, and for some time past, while the low price of wheat discouraged the existing wheat trade there, it has been found profitable to export barley from the Gulf ports. Barley is the cheapest grain in Persia, where it is grown for home consumption only, being the universal food for horses. Owing to want of care with the seed, and the close vicinity of crops, the wheat was often so mixed with barley as to reduce the price considerably, and the question of mixture and reduction was always a very stormy one. When I was at Ahwaz, on the Karun, in 1890, I saw a machine at work separating the grains, and the Arab owners waiting to take away the unsaleable barley, the wheat being bought for export by a European firm there which owned the machine. The Arab sellers probably now move to the other side of the machine to carry away the unsaleable wheat, the barley being bought for export owing to the turn of trade.

The German group that has obtained the Persian road concession has also taken up the old project of an extension of the Tehran tramways to the villages on the slopes of the Shimran range, all within a distance of ten miles from the town. The Court, the city notables, and the foreign legations, with everyone who desires to be fashionable, and can afford the change, reside there during the warm months-- June, July, August and September. The whole place may be described as the summer suburb of the capital, and there is great going to and fro.

I have already mentioned the Russian road now under construction from the Caspian Sea base to Kasvin, with the object of enabling Russian trade to command more thoroughly the Tehran market. The total distance from the coast to the capital is two hundred miles. There is an old-established caravan track over easy country, from Kasvin to Hamadan in the south--west, distant about one hundred and fifty miles. It has lately been announced that the Russian Road Company has obtained a concession to convert this track into a cart-road in continuation of that from Resht. It is seen that with improved communication Russian trade may be made to compete successfully at Hamadan, which is only about fifty miles further from the Caspian Sea base than Tehran, and there will also be the advantage of a return trade in cotton from Central Persia, as Armenian merchants now export it to Russia from as far South as Isfahan and Yezd. The German road from Baghdad to Tehran will be met at Hamadan.

Kermanshah and Hamadan, through which the German road will pass, are both busy centres of trade in districts rich in corn, wool, and wine. They are also meeting-points of the great and ever-flowing streams of pilgrims to Kerbela *via* Baghdad, said to number annually about one hundred thousand. This has been a popular pilgrim route, as well as trade route, for centuries, and with greater facilities on an improved road the traffic is certain to increase.

It is said that the alignment of the Russian road from Resht is to be made in view of a railway in the future. The same will probably be done in the Hamadan extension, and it is believed that the German road will be similarly planned. All this would mean that behind the concessions are further promises for the time when railway construction comes. Looking into the dim distance, the eye of faith and hope may see the fulfilment of railway communication from India to Europe by a connection between the Quetta or Indus Valley line and Kermanshah.

This brings us to the agreement of 1890 between Persia and Russia to shut out railways till the end of the century. This agreement, when made known, was regarded as proof of a somewhat barbarian policy on the part of Russia, unwilling or unable herself to assist in opening up Persia and improving the condition of the country. But there is some reason for the idea that the Shah himself was ready to meet the Russian request, so as to keep back the railway which he feared would soon connect his capital with the Caucasus. There was much railway talk in Persia in 1890, and Russia knew that it would take quite ten years to complete her railway system up to the Northern frontiers of Persia and Afghanistan. The railway now being made from Tiflis to Alexandropol and Kars will probably send out a line down the fertile valley of the Aras to Julfa, ready for extension across the Persian frontier to Tabriz, and a branch may be pushed forward from Doshakh, or Keribent, on the Trans-Caspian railway, to Sarakhs, where Russia, Persia, and Afghanistan meet, to facilitate trade with Herat as well as Meshed. In the meanwhile also the cart-roads, ready for railway purposes if wanted, from the Caspian Sea base to Kasvin, Tehran, and Hamadan, will be completed.

Russia insisted on regarding the opening of the Karun to the navigation of the world as a diplomatic victory for England, and a distinct concession to British commerce, which is predominant in the South. She therefore thought out well what to get from the Shah in return, to favour her commercial policy in the North, and the ten years' prohibition of railways was the result. Russia desires commercial predominance in Persia just as England does, and she will use all the influence which her dominating close neighbourhood gives to obtain the utmost favour and facilities for her trade.

While Russia and England were thus engaged in strong commercial rivalry, Germany unexpectedly made her appearance in the Western region of Central Persia, where their competition meets. Nor has Persia been idle in trading enterprise; her merchants are not only aiming at getting more exclusively into their own hands the interior commerce of the country, but they have established direct relations with firms in foreign countries, and now work in active competition with the European houses which in old days had almost all the export and import trade in their own hands. The introduction of the Imperial Bank of Persia has given an impetus to this new spirit of native enterprise by affording facilities which before were not available on the same favourable terms. The Nasiri Company, a mercantile corporation of Persians, was formed in 1889 to trade on the Karun, and it commenced operations with two small steamers. Later, a third steamer was added, and they are now negotiating for the purchase of a fourth. They have a horse tramway, about one and a half miles long, to facilitate the necessary transhipment of cargo between the upper and lower streams, where the Ahwaz Rapids break the river navigation. This trading corporation has strong support, and the Persian Government is earnest in giving it every assistance, so that it may develop into an effectual agency for the revival of the prosperity which made the Karun Valley in old times what the Nile Valley is now.

Messrs. Lynch Brothers also run a large steamer on the Lower Karun in connection with a 'stern-wheeler' (Nile boat pattern) on the upper stream, and between them and the Nasiri Company a regular and quick communication is maintained between Bombay and Shuster. One of the articles of import at the latter place is American kerosene-oil for lamp purposes, to take the place of the Shuster crude petroleum, said to have been used there for centuries. This petroleum contains an unusual amount of benzine, and being highly explosive in lamps, the Shuster people, who can afford to pay for the safer substance, have taken to American oil. The Shuster petroleum-springs belong to a family of Syuds in the town, and did not fall within the field of the Persian Mines Corporation. These oil-springs may yet become the object of practical operations should the Nasiri Company develop the resources of the Karun Valley.

Belgium has also taken an active interest in Persia lately, the tramway company, and the glass manufactory at Tehran, and the beet-sugar factory in the vicinity, having all been established with Belgian capital; and Holland, who is believed to be seeking an opening in Persia, may find her opportunity in the Karun Valley irrigation works. The creation of strong international interests in Persia should have the best effect in strengthening her national independence, developing her natural resources, and introducing good government. And the peaceful succession of the lawful heir to the throne should go far to carry the country forward in the path of progress and prosperity. It is evident that the strong sentiment attaching to the late Shah's long and peaceful reign, and the popular feeling of loyalty to him which influenced the people, has had the effect of enforcing the royal will in favour of the heir legitimately appointed by Nasr-ed-Din Shah.

The reigning family of Persia are the hereditary chiefs of the royal Kajar tribe, and still preserve the customs of that position. They have not changed the manly habits of a warlike race for the luxury and lethargy which sapped the energies and ruined the lives of so many monarchs of Persia. Up to the time of the present ruling dynasty the princes of the blood were immured in the harem, where their education was left to women and their attendants, and until the death of the King his destined successor was not known. At that period the son of the lowest slave in the harem was deemed equally eligible to succeed to the throne with the offspring of the proudest princess who boasted the honour of marriage with the Sovereign. And similarly as in the West, up to about four hundred years ago, the Crown was generally made secure by murder, every actual or possible rival for the throne being blinded or removed from the scene. This was the practice of the Soffivean dynasty, which preceded the Kajar. But with the change which then took place, this hideous practice disappeared, and usages more congenial to the feelings of the military tribes which support the throne were established. Under the late Shah the princes of the blood were employed in the chief governments of the country, and exercised all the powers and responsibilities of office.

Persia may be described as a theocratic democracy under an absolute monarchy. There is no hereditary rank but that of royal birth, and that of the chiefs of the military tribes, who may be regarded as a military aristocracy; but there is a system of life titles which secure to the holders certain privileges and immunities, and are much prized. The titles are nominally descriptive of some personal quality, talent, or trust, such as Councillor of the State, Confidant of the King, Trusted of the Sultan; they are also bestowed upon ladies in high position. The name of an animal is never introduced into the title; at least, I have only heard of one instance to the contrary in modern times. An individual of European parentage was recommended to the late Shah's notice and favour by his Persian patrons, and they mentioned his great wish to be honoured with a title. His Majesty, who had a keen sense of humour, observed the suggestive appearance of the candidate for honours, and said, 'Well, he is Hujabr-i-Mulk' (the Lion of the Country). The new noble was ready with his grateful thanks: 'Your sacred Majesty, may I be thy sacrifice;' but he added in a subdued tone, 'A lion requires at least a lamb a day.' The Shah laughed at the meaning speech, and said, 'Let him have it.' The granting of a title does not give any emolument unless specially directed. As a precedent for this title, the Shah may have had in his mind the story of Ali Kuli Khan, one of the favourites of Shah Suliman. During the reign of Shah Abbas this chief was generally in prison, except when his services were required against the enemies of his country. This had gained for him the name of the Lion of Persia, as men said that he was always chained except when wanted to fight.

The Shah can raise whomsoever he chooses from the lowest to the highest position or post, except in the most powerful of the nomad tribes, where the nomination to chieftainship is confined to the elders of the leading families, who generally represent two lines from one head, one being in the opposition when the other is in power. The chieftain of a clan considers himself superior in real rank to the most favoured Court title-holder, and the chiefs of the military tribes may be termed the hereditary nobility of Persia. The monarch may, by his influence or direct power, alter the succession, and place an uncle in the situation of a nephew, and sometimes a younger brother in the condition of an elder, but the leader of the tribe must be of the family of their chief. The younger sons and nephews are enrolled in the royal guard, and the Shah is thus enabled by judicious change and selection to keep his hold upon the tribe. Change of chiefs is not always effected peacefully. The wild tribesmen who, in feudal fashion, attach themselves as idle men-at-arms to a popular leader are sometimes disinclined to accept his fall from favour without an appeal to arms. But the royal authority prevails in the end, and the new chiefs rule begins, and lasts just so long as Fortune smiles and the Shah wills.

A marked instance of this was shown in July, 1892, when Jehan Shah Khan-Ilbegi was deprived of the chieftaincy of the Afshar section of the powerful Shahsevend tribe, who range from Ardebil to Tehran. The famous Nadir Shah was originally a simple trooper of this tribe, and belonged to the colony of it which was planted at Deregez on the Turkoman border. The ostensible cause of the chiefs removal from power was that with his own hands he had killed his wife, the sister of his cousin, Rahmat-ulla-Khan, who was known to be his rival in the tribe for place and power. Jehan Shah had unjustly accused her of being unfaithful to him, and going to her house, he called her out, and, notwithstanding her appearing with a copy of the Sacred Koran in her hand, shot her dead while in the act of swearing on the holy book that she was innocent of all guilt. Jehan Shah than went in search of the tribesman whom he suspected of being her paramour, and killed him also. The matter was reported to the Shah, then in camp in Irak, who ordered Jebam Shah to be deprived of the chieftainship, and Rahmat-ulla-Khan to be appointed Ilbegi in his place. It was further ordered that Jehan Shah should be arrested and sent as a prisoner to Tehran. The Ihtisham-e-Dowleh-Kajar, cousin of the late Shah and Governor of Khamseh, in which province Jehan Shah was then located with his clan, was directed to carry out the royal commands.

Much telegraphing had taken place on the subject, and as cipher was not used, Jehan Shah, by means of money and influence, was able to obtain the fullest information of all that passed, and as he was known to have a numerous personal following armed with Peabody-Martini rifles, the Governor was instructed to act with caution. He accordingly had recourse to stratagem, and gave out that the object of his journey to the tribal quarters was to coerce a section of the tribe which had been giving trouble. He therefore asked Jehan Shah to assist him, and this gave the chief a good excuse for assembling his men. The Prince Governor took with him one hundred cavalry and four hundred infantry, but no attention was paid to the ammunition, and they started without a proper supply.

Rahmat-ulla-Khan was fully aware of the Governor's real intentions, but the influence and power of the popular chief prevented any partisan gathering against him. He therefore could only depend upon the Persian troops to enforce the order of the Shah, and was unable to do more than prepare a reception tent and provide a luncheon for the Prince and his people, about eight miles in advance of their camp, at a place appointed for the meeting with himself and Jehan Shah. On approaching this place, these two, with the elders and the tribesmen, went forward for the customary ceremonial reception of the Governor. Jehan Shah dismounted and saluted with the utmost show of respect; but on reaching the tent which had been prepared for them by his rival, he declined to enter and partake of his hospitality, declaring that he preferred to pass on to his own tents, some distance off, his mounted following of fifteen hundred men accompanying him. The Governor knew that Jehan Shah had become dangerous from the devotion of his well-armed followers, and the readiness of the main body of the fierce fighting tribesmen to support him. He had evidently contemplated his arrest and seizure at the place of meeting, but the show of force and feeling in Jehan Shah's favour was too strong to admit of any such attempt. He therefore decided to declare openly the object of his coming, and after lunch he assembled the elders of the tribe, and summoned Jehan Shah to his presence, who, however, declined to obey. The Prince on this announced his deposition, and the appointment of Rahmat-ulla-Khan in his place, showing at the same time the Shah's written commands. He then appears to have indulged in some violent abuse of Jehan Shah, and again sent an order to secure his presence.

In the meanwhile, that chief had taken counsel with his tribal following, numbering about fifteen hundred, armed with breechloaders, and finding them entirely on his side, and determined to dispute the rule of his rival, he served out cartridges freely, and decided to discuss the matter with the Governor. He left most of his men at some distance, and presented himself attended by only a few. The Prince informed him of the Shah's orders, and after some contentious talk, he held out the royal firman for him or any of those with him to read. On one of the elders moving forward to take the paper, Jehan Shah suddenly motioned them all back with his hands, and the Prince, taking alarm at this appearance of a signal, called out to his guards to seize Jehan Shah. There was a shout and a rush, and some of Jehan Shah's men from behind fired over the heads of the soldiers, who, however, returned the fire point-blank, killing and wounding several of the Shahsevends. The tribesmen then opened fire in earnest, and the Prince with his troops promptly fled. All ran and rode for their lives, pursued by the furious enemy. Some of the servants kept with their master, and remounted him twice when the horses he rode were wounded and disabled. The tribesmen are said to have made him a special target, for he was most conspicuous in rich dress, and a third time he and his horse were rolled over together, he receiving two bullet-wounds. He was then seized, partially stripped, and treated with great indignity. The pursuit was kept up to his camp, which was captured and plundered; thirty-five of his men were killed, and fifty wounded. One of the Prince's officials, also wounded, was taken with him, and both were kept prisoners for three days.

In the meantime Jehan Shah, having recovered from his mad fury, trembled at the recollection of his crime, and dreading the vengeance which he saw was certain to follow, he packed up his valuables and fled with a few followers to the Caspian coast. He had the intention to escape by steamer to Baku, but failing in this, owing to all communication with Russian territory having been suspended during the outbreak of cholera then prevailing, he determined to make his way by land across the Northern frontier. Being closely pursued by a party of Persian cavalry, he abandoned all his baggage, and with great difficulty reached Tabriz, where he was constrained to take sanctuary in the house of the chief Moulla. He died there after enduring existence for about six months under circumstances and with surroundings which must have been supremely hateful to him. I was at Tabriz in the end of 1892, while he was there, and I was told by one who had seen him that he was a sad sight then, the hereditary head of the Afshar Shahsevends, a section of a royal tribe, herding in misery with a crowd of criminals seeking sanctuary in order to avoid the avenger of blood. On the first news of the occurrence the Shah ordered the immediate mobilization of the infantry regiments of Khamseh and Kasvin, and this had the effect of dispersing the tribe, facilitating the work of retribution, and establishing the power of the new chief. This incident had the best political result in aiding the Kajar policy of breaking up the ruling families and the cohesion of the dangerous tribes, and asserting fully the authority of the Tehran Central Government. Jehan Shah had gradually improved and strengthened his position by increasing the superior armament of his tribesmen (who were said to have three thousand breechloaders) and laying in a large supply of cartridges, so that, with his wealth, influence, and popularity, he must have been regarded as dangerously powerful. No doubt the conceited confidence thus produced led him to indulge in the ungovernable rage which wrecked his freedom and ended his life. The tribesmen said that the wife whom he killed was truly innocent; but being themselves men of wild ways and tempestuous temper, they thought he had been harshly judged, and they therefore stood by him to resist his seizure and deportation.

As in England four hundred years ago, every place of worship is a sacred refuge; and the dwelling-house of the Chief Priest gives similar protection. This right of sanctuary continues in force throughout Persia; but to benefit by it for any length of time, money is very necessary, for without such aid, or when the supplies fail, starvation steps in to drive the refugee out. While in sanctuary, compromise and arrangement may be effected, so that the fugitive may be allowed to go unmolested, the relatives paying, or becoming 'bail' for, the blood-money or compensation agreed upon. A fugitive from justice, oppression, or revenge often claims the privilege of sanctuary in the house or premises of a local dignitary of influence, whose house would not be unceremoniously entered by pursuers, and this affords time either to meet the demands or accusations made, or to escape to a safer place.

At Tehran there is a big gun, said to have been brought by Nadir Shah from Delhi, and known as the Pearl Cannon. It is said to be so called from having had a string of pearls hung on it near the muzzle when it was on show in Imperial Delhi. This was probably the case, for we know that heavy guns in India were regarded with a degree of respect and reverence almost approaching worship. The gunners of the Maharajah Runjeet Singh, the Lion of the Punjab, used to 'salaam' to their guns, and to hang garlands of the sweet-scented *champak* flower, which is used in temples and at festivals, round the muzzles. The Pearl Cannon occupies a prominent position close to the Shah's palace, and has always been recognised as possessing a semi-sacred character, and giving the right of sanctuary to those who touch it and remain by it.

I remember a regiment of infantry, represented by three hundred men who were 'off duty' and available for the demonstration, claiming the privilege of this great gun sanctuary after they had assailed the house of their Colonel in order to wreak their vengeance on him, as he was suspected of withholding their pay. The officer's servants were warned in time, and closed the courtyard door, so that the rioters were unable to enter; but they relieved their feelings by battering the door with stones and damaging the Colonel's carriage, which they found outside. Having thus created a great disturbance and excited considerable rumour, they proceeded to the Pearl Cannon, and gave vent to their grievances in loud cries, which reached the royal palace, on which the Shah, Nasr-ed-Din, was made acquainted with all the facts, and caused the soldiers' wrongs to be redressed. One of the charges against the Colonel was that he had managed, by lending money to the men, to gain possession of their village lands by unfair means--for he was a landlord in the same district, and desired to add to his holding. The corps was the Larajani territorial infantry battalion, and an English resident at Tehran, who caught the name as Larry-Johnny, said the whole incident was 'quite Irish, you know.'

CHAPTER V.

--The military tribes and the royal guard --Men of the people as great monarchs --Persian sense of humour --Nightingales and poetry --Legendary origin of the royal emblem --Lion and Sun --Ancient Golden Eagle emblem --The Blacksmith's Apron the royal standard.

The warlike nomads form a most important part of the military strength of Persia, and it has always been the policy of the Sovereign to secure their personal attachment to him as the direct paramount chief of each martial clan. In pursuance of this policy, the royal guard, known as Gholam-i-Shah, or Slaves of the King, which protects and escorts the Shah in camp and quarters, is mainly composed of bodies of horse furnished from the best and most powerful of the military tribes. These come from all quarters of the empire, and are headed and officered by members of the most influential families, so that they may be regarded as hostages for the loyalty and fidelity of the chiefs. All are changed from time to time, and thus a system of short service prevails, to give as many as possible a term of duty with the royal guard.

The term *gholam*, or slave, has always been given as a title to the personal guards, and everyone who is admitted to the corps claims the envied distinction of Gholam-i-Shah. This guard has a very ancient origin, and service in it is highly prized as giving opportunities of attracting the attention and gaining the favour of the King. The great Sovereign Sabuktagin, who reigned in the tenth century, was said to have risen from the ranks of the royal guard. All the couriers of the foreign legations at Tehran are styled Gholam, and the title is accepted as an honourable one, meaning a mounted servant of courage and trust, who is ready to defend to the death all interests committed to his charge.

The total strength of 'the guard' is twelve hundred and fifty, of whom two hundred are the elite, called gholam peshkhidmet (personal attendants) and mostly belong to the Kajar, the Shah's own tribe, with which his Majesty always identified himself in the most public manner, and thus made every man proud of his clanship with the King. I here allude to the royal signature, 'Nasr-ed-Din, Shah, Kajar.' These superior guardsmen have all the rank of gentleman, and may be called the mounted 'gentlemen at arms' of the guard. They have the customary right of appointment to Court and palace posts, such as door-keeper, usher, messenger, etc. Their service is for life, and is hereditary, a son succeeding his father, and taking his place in the guard when promotion, age, illness, or death creates a vacancy. They have distinctive horse-trappings with silver neck-straps, breastplates, and headstalls, which pass from father to son, and have become highly prized heirlooms. The Shah was most partial to the representative tribesmen of his guard, and his happy characteristics as a King of nomadic taste and camp-like ways, in familiar acquaintance with all about him, were well shown at a military review which I witnessed at Tehran some years ago. The review was a special one, held in honour of the Swedish officers deputed by King Oscar II. of Norway and Sweden to convey the high order of the Seraphin to his Majesty the Shah, and as many troops as possible were called in from the surrounding districts to take part in it. The royal guard mustered strong, and when they marched past, the Shah stepped forward to the saluting line, so as to be closer to them, and called out to each troop, and named each commander in terms of praise and pleasure. This display of personal knowledge of the men, and acquaintance with their leaders, drew from them a perfect buzz of delight.

On this occasion the smart appearance of the Bakhtiari horse attracted particular attention. The Persian bystanders showed their pride in these popular mounted mountaineers by the admiring exclamation, 'Here come the Bakhtiaris!' They were very noticeable by their white felt, round, brimless hats, and the good line they preserved when passing. The Bakhtiaris (Lurs) are the most numerous and powerful of all the military tribes, and are noted for their superior martial qualities both as horse and foot. They are of the most ancient Persian descent, and have held the hills and valleys of Luristan from time immemorial; while all the other military tribes may be said to be of much later date, and of foreign origin--Arab, Syrian, Turk, and Tartar. Competent authorities, who have had full opportunity of judging, agree in saying that they are as good material for soldiers as can be found anywhere. I was greatly interested in hearing the Shah's Prime Minister speak in glowing terms of the gallantry of the Bakhtiari infantry at the capture of Kandahar under Nadir Shah, who, after subduing them in their own mountains, won them over to serve him loyally and well in his conquering campaigns against Afghanistan and India. The Grand Vizier mentioned the circumstance of the Bakhtiari contingent, after one of the many repulses met in the repeated attempts to carry Kandahar by storm, having in the evening, when all was quiet on both sides, assaulted without orders and captured a commanding, position in the defences, which they had failed to take during the day. The shouts of the victors roused the resting besiegers, and Nadir at once took advantage of the success to carry the citadel and gain possession of the town. As a closing remark concerning these nomad tribes, I may mention that they regard themselves as in every way superior to the settled inhabitants, and express this conceit in their saying, 'One man of the tents is equal to two of the town.'

I have mentioned the prerogative of the Shah to raise whomsoever he chooses from the lowest to the highest position, except under restrictions in the military tribes. This quite falls in with the democratic spirit which lies dormant among the people, ready to be displayed in willingness to accept a Sovereign of signal power who springs from the lower ranks of life. The social equality which Islam grants to all men was nothing new to Persia in forming ideas regarding a popular leader and elected King. The descent of such a man is deemed of little consequence in the minds of a people who look to personification of power as the right to rule. In fact, with them it is said that the fame of such a man is in proportion to the lowness of his origin. They know of notable instances of the nation being delivered from terrible tyranny and degrading foreign subjection, and being made gloriously great, by men of the people. They point to Kawah, the blacksmith, who headed a revolt against the monstrously cruel usurper King Zohak, using his apron as a banner, and finally overthrew and slew him, and placed Faridun, a Prince of the Peshdadian dynasty, on the throne which he might have occupied himself. This blacksmith's apron continued for ages to be the royal standard of Persia. In the ninth century, Yacub-bin-Leis, called the Pewterer, as he had worked when young at that (his father's) trade, made his way to the throne by sheer force of strong character and stout courage. He remained the people's hero to the last, was noted for his simple habits, for keeping with his name his trade appellation (Suffari, the Pewterer), and for never having been wantonly cruel or oppressive. In the tenth century, when the great Sabuktagin rose from soldier to Sovereign, we see the principle of selection in preference to hereditary succession practised and accepted by the nation. And the choice was justified by the glory he gave to the Persian arms in extending the empire to India, and in the further conquests of his soldier-son, Mahmud, who succeeded to his father's throne, and added still more to the greatness of the kingdom, till it reached from Baghdad to Kashgar, from Georgia to Bengal, from the Oxus to the Ganges.

When the country was groaning under the Afghan yoke, it was the daring spirit of one from the ranks of the people, Nadir Kuli (Shah), who conceived the overthrow of the oppressor and the recovery of Persian independence. Originally a simple trooper of the Afshar tribe, he advanced himself by valour, boldness, and enterprise, and crowned his successes by winning the admiration of the royal leaders and adherents, who on the death of the infant King, Abbas III., son of Shah Tamasp, elected him to be their King. As such he carried the war into the country of the evicted oppressors, and established the power of the empire from the Oxus to Delhi, whence he returned with the splendid spoil which yet enriches and adorns the Crown of Persia. It speaks much for Nadir Shah's strong character that, having gained such distinction, he did not allow flatterers to find amid the obscurity of his birth the lost traces of great ancestors. He never boasted a proud genealogy; on the contrary, he often spoke of his low birth, and we are told that even his flattering historian had to content himself with saying that the diamond has its value from its own lustre, and not from the rock in which it grows. A characteristic story of this remarkable man is that on demanding a daughter of his vanquished enemy, Mahmud Shah, the Emperor of Delhi, in marriage for his son, Nasr-ullah, he was met with the answer that for alliance with a Princess of the Imperial house of Timor a genealogy of seven generations was required. 'Tell him,' said Nadir, 'that Nasr-ullah is the son of Nadir Shah, the son of the sword, the grandson of the sword, and so on till they have a descent of seventy, instead of seven generations.' Nadir, the man of action and blood and iron, had the greatest contempt for the weak, dissolute Mahmud Shah, who, according to the native historian of the time, was 'never without a mistress in his arms and a glass in his hand,' a debauchee of the lowest type, as well as a mere puppet King. In the end the demon of suspicion poisoned the mind of

Nadir to such an extent that he became madly murderous, and assassination ended his life. The Persians say that he began as a deliverer and ended as a destroyer.

As a people, the Persians are of a happy disposition and bright imagination, doubtless produced by the dry, clear air of their high tableland, which relieves from dullness and depression. They enjoy a joke and laugh heartily, and they are able to see that most things have their comic side. The late Shah was quick to show the merry look of appreciation when something amusing was said. At the Nauroz Court reception of the Corps Diplomatique all the Legations, headed by the Turkish Embassy, were ranged in a semicircle in front of the Shah, and after the congratulatory address was delivered by the Sultan's Ambassador, his Majesty advanced and walked round slowly, pausing to say a few words to each Minister. His face lit up with animation when he spoke to one whom he knew to be able to reply in the Persian tongue. On one occasion, after speaking with the Ottoman Ambassador, who is always a Persian linguist (Persian being an obligatory subject of qualification for the Tehran post), he passed on to a Minister who was a good Persian scholar. Further on he found an equally well--qualified colloquial proficient in another; and on finding himself before a well-known very clever diplomatist for whom he had a great personal liking, he smiled and said pleasantly, 'Have you learnt any Persian yet?' The Minister bowed, and, looking duly serious, said in Persian, 'I know something.' The Minister meant to say that he knew a little, but the word 'something,' as used, could be taken, as in English, to signify 'a thing or two.' Such a meaning from the diplomatist who spoke was quite appropriate, and the Shah laughed softly and looked much amused.

As another instance (but in this case of grim humour) of seeing the comic side, a Prince Governor of a province, sitting in judgment, ordered a merchant to pay a fine of fifty tomans, but, though well known to be rich, he protested his utter inability to pay, saying he had never seen such a sum of money, and begged for some other punishment which the Prince in his wisdom and mercy would command. His Highness then suggested a choice of eating fifty raw onions, or eating fifty sticks (the Oriental mode of expression when speaking of bastinado strokes), or paying the fifty tomans. Persians are fond of raw onions, those they eat being small, and the merchant enjoyed the prospect of thus saving his money. He thought that the punishment had been ordered in ignorance, so, concealing his feeling of happy surprise, and affecting fear, he elected for onions. He struggled hard with them, but could not swallow more than half the number. He was then asked to pay the fine, but he claimed his further choice of the fifty sticks. Triced up, he underwent the pain of twenty-five well laid on to the soles of his feet, and then called out that he would willingly pay the fifty tomans to have no more. On this he was cast loose, and the Prince said, 'You fool! you had a choice of one of three punishments, and you took all three.'

Persian servants regard their fixed pay as but a retaining fee, and look for their real wages in perquisites. They show considerable ingenuity and brightness of idea in reasons for purchasing this, that, and the other thing, not really required, but affording opportunities for 'pickings.' A new head-servant, on looking round his master's premises, and seeing no opening for a fresh purchase, at last cast his eye on the fowls, kept to secure a supply of fresh eggs, instead of the doubtful ones bought in the bazaar. He introduced stale eggs into the fowl-house, and on their condition being remarked at breakfast, he gravely explained that he had noticed the hens were old, and it sometimes happened that old hens laid stale eggs, whereas young hens always laid fresh eggs; so he suggested clearing out the fowl-house and restocking it with young poultry.

The leisure time the servants have is not always well spent, it is true, but they have ideas of imagination and sentiment, which in some degree is suggestive of refinement. I have seen this shown in their love of singing birds, and their dandy ways of dress; for some of them are very particular as to the cut of a coat and the fit of a hat. I have sometimes been interested in seeing them carefully tending their pet nightingales, cleaning the cages, and decking them out with bits of coloured cloth and any flowers in season. In November I saw quite a dozen cages thus brightened, each with its brisk-looking nightingale occupant, put out in the sunshine in the courtyard; and on asking about such a collection of cages, was told rather shyly, as if fearing a smile at their sentimental ways, that there was an afternoon tea that day in the neighbourhood, to which the nightingales and their owners were going. These singing-bird-parties are held in the underground rooms of houses, which are cool in summer and warm in winter, and I imagine the company and rivalry of a number of birds in the semi-darkness, with glimmering light from the 'kalian' pipes, and the bubbling of water in the pipe-bowls, and the boiling samovar tea-urns, all combine to cheat the birds pleasantly into believing that it is night-time in the spring song-season.

The Persian poets brought the nightingale much into their songs of praise of earthly joys. The bulbul, of which they wrote and sang, was the European nightingale, which visits Persia in spring to sing and love and nest. They pass as far South as Shiraz, where they meet the plump little Indian bulbul, which is often mistaken for the Shiraz poets' singing-bird. The word is applied to both species in India and Persia, but the birds are quite different in shape, plumage, and voice. They meet at Shiraz, a place which possesses a climate so temperate and equable as to bring together the birds and fruits of the East and West, North and South; for there I saw and heard the Indian bulbul and the hoopoe, the European nightingale, the cuckoo, and the magpie, and I know that the fruits range from apples to dates.

The nightingale is the favourite pet singing-bird of the Persians. I had good information regarding the manner of obtaining them for cage purposes from some small boys who were engaged picking roses in a rose-garden at Ujjatabod, near Yezd. There are two large rose-gardens in that oasis in the Yezd Desert, where the manufacture of rose-water and the attar essence is carried on. The gardens are appropriately favourite haunts of the nightingales on their return with the season of gladness from their winter resorts in the woods of the Caspian coast. The Persian poets tell of the passionate love of the nightingale for the scented rose, and in fanciful figure of speech make the full-blossomed flower complain of too much kissing from its bird-lover, so that its sweetness goes, and its beauty fades far too sadly soon. The boys told me of the number of family pairs, their nests and eggs, and said that they took the young male birds when fully fledged and about to leave the nest, and brought them up by hand at first, till able to feed themselves. There is a great demand in the towns for the young nightingales, which in Persia sing well in captivity, so rarely the case with the bird in Europe. The shopkeepers like to have their pet birds by them, and in the nesting season they may be heard all over the bazaars, singing sweetly and longingly for the partners they know of by instinct, but never meet.

There is much pleasing romance and sentiment in the popular idea regarding the origin of the national emblem, Sher o Khurshed (the Lion and the Sun). The following legend concerning it was told to me by the Malik-ut-Tujjar, or Master of the Merchants of Tehran, a gentleman well versed in Persian history, literature, and lore, and who spoke with all the enthusiasm of national pride. When the first monarchy of Ajam (Persia) was founded by Kai Uramas, some five thousand years ago, the sun was in the sign of Asad (Leo), the highest tower in the heavens, and the lion was therefore taken as the Persian emblem, and it so remained without the sun over it, as now shown, till about six hundred years ago. Ghazan Khan, who then reigned as King, was so attached to his wife, the Queen Khurshed (the Sun), that he desired to perpetuate her name by putting it on the coins he struck; but the Ulema objected to a woman's name on the King's coin, whereupon he decided to put her face on a rising sun above the national emblem of the lion, as now seen in the well-known royal arms of Persia. The story is that King Ghazan's affection for his Queen, Khurshed, was such that he styled her Sham'bu Ghazan (the Light of Ghazan).

This may have been the origin of the expression Khurshed Kullah, or Sun-crowned, which I have seen stated is a term that was used to denote the Sovereign of an empire, but from the fact of the features and style of dressing the hair shown in the sun-picture being those of a woman, I think the title may be regarded as applied only to queens. Catherine II. of Russia, from the magnificence of her Court, her beauty and ambition, and her fame in love and war, was known in Persia during her lifetime as Khurshed Kullah, and she is still designated by that title.

I would here mention another instance of a Mohammedan monarch desiring to publish to his people in the most sovereign manner his high regard for a wife by putting her name on the current coin. The reign of the Emperor Jehangir, son of Akbar the Great, the founder of the Moghul Empire in India and the builder of Agra, was chiefly remarkable for the influence exercised over him by his favourite wife, Nur Mahal, the Light of the Harem, immortalized by Moore in 'Lalla Rookh.' The currency was struck in her name, and we are also told that in her hands centred all the intrigues that make up the work of Oriental administration. She lies buried by the side of her husband at Lahore, the capital of the Punjab.

The subject of Ghazan Khan's succession to the throne of Persia is an unusually interesting one. He was a Moghul chief of the line of Chengiz Khan, and, holding Persia in tributary dependence for his sovereign master the Khakan, was at the head of one hundred thousand tried Tartar warriors. Persia was then Mohammedan, and the proposal was made to him to join the new faith, and become the King-elect of an independent Iran. He consulted his commanders, and then decided to enter Islam and become King. His apostasy was followed by the instant conversion of his hundred thousand men, who, with the true spirit of Tartar soldiers, followed their leader into the pale of Islam, and soon became the active supporters of the faith which they had so suddenly embraced. We can imagine the triumphant joy of the proselytizing priests as they passed down the crowded ranks of the time-hardened, weather-proof warrior sons of the bow and spear, who on June 17, 1265, paraded at Firozkoh, where the Tartar host was then encamped, to repeat the Mohammedan confession of faith. To them the learning of the Arabic words must have been the severest exercise they had ever been called upon to practise, and it is easy to think of the muttered swearing among the puzzled veterans that what was good enough for their leader was good enough for them, and that they were ready to do as he had done, without further talk or ceremony. Islam was then most actively aggressive, extending by the argument of smooth speech or sharp sword, as occasion demanded, and the Moullas must have regarded with enthusiastic pride the glorious reinforcement they had brought to its armies by the consecration of such a splendid warrior host to the service of their Church.

Ghazan Khan was the first of this race of kings from the line of Chengiz who threw off all allegiance to Tartary by directing that the name of the monarch of that empire should not in future be put on the Persian coins. On the coins which he struck, the Mohammedan creed, 'There is no God but God, and Mohammed is His Prophet,' was inscribed instead of the name and titles of the Khakan. He had not the courage of his heart's desire to strike his wife's name on the coins, as Jehangir did, but he was differently placed, in that, as a fresh convert and a new King by the favour of Islam, he felt himself unable to put aside the priests who had bribed him with a crown. Malcolm, in remarking on Ghazan Khan's accession to the throne of Persia, says that Henry IV. of France similarly changed his creed to secure the crown.

Ghazan Khan reigned about the middle of the thirteenth century, and was known in Europe for his supposed readiness to assist in re-establishing the Christians in the Holy Land. He was deemed a wise and just Prince, and it is believed that his policy led him to seek the aid of the States of Europe in order to improve the position and condition of himself and his kingdom. It is said that Pope Boniface

VIII endeavoured by a display of his connection with Ghazan Khan to excite the Christian princes to another Crusade, and it was probably this connection with the head of the Christian Church which led to a general impression among Western writers that Ghazan Khan was not sincere in his conversion to Mohammedanism, and was at heart a Christian. There is reason to think that the secret spring of his action was to weaken the Egyptian Empire, which he regarded as hostile and dangerous to himself and Persia. It is not clear whether Ghazan Khan apostatized from the religion of his ancestors or that of the Christians, but he is believed to have been attached all his life to the latter faith, though he does not appear to have made a public declaration of his belief in its doctrines. He professed Mohammedanism in order to obtain the crown, but his life had been passed in friendship with Christians, and in wars with the followers of the faith he adopted.

Xenophon mentions that the royal emblem of Persia from early times was a golden eagle with outstretched wings, resting on a spearhead like the Roman eagle, but he makes no allusion to a standard. Persian historians tell of a famous standard carried from the mythical time of Zohak to that of the last of the Pehlevi kings. Their story is that Kawah, a blacksmith, raised a successful revolt against the implacably cruel King Zohak in the earliest time of Persian sovereignty, and relieved the country from his terrible tyranny by putting him to death. The victorious blacksmith then placed on the throne Faridun, a Prince of the Peshdadian dynasty, who adopted his apron, which had been the standard of revolt, as the royal banner of Persia. As such it was said to be richly ornamented with jewels, to which every king, from Faridun to the last of the Pehlevi monarchs, added. It was called the Durafsh-i-Kawah (the Standard of Kawah), and continued to be the royal standard of Persia till the Mohammedan conquest, when it was taken in battle by Saad-e-Wakass, and sent to the Khalif Omar. Malcolm said that the causes which led to the sign of Sol in Leo becoming the arms of Persia could not be distinctly traced, but thought there was reason to believe that the use of this symbol was not of very great antiquity. He said, with reference to it being upon the coins of one of the Seljukian dynasty of Iconium, that when this family was destroyed by Halaku, the grandson of Chengiz, it was far from improbable that that Prince or his successor adopted this emblematical representation as a trophy of his conquest, and that it has remained ever since among the most remarkable of the royal insignia of Persia. He also mentioned the opinion that this representation of Sol in Leo was first adopted by Ghiat-u-din-Kai-Khusru-bin-Kai-Kobad, 1236 A.D., and that the emblem is supposed to have reference either to his own horoscope or that of his Queen, who was a Princess of Georgia. This approaches the legend told by the Malik-ut-Tujjar of Tehran, for the face depicted on Sol is that of a woman.

CHAPTER VI.

--The Order of the Lion and the Sun --Rex and Dido --Dervishes --Endurance of Persian horses --The Shah's stables --The sanctuary of the stable --Long distance races --A country of horses --The *gymkhana* in Tehran --Olive industry near Resht --Return journey --Grosnoje oil-field --Russian railway travelling --Improved communication with Tehran.

The distinguished Persian Order of the Lion and the Sun was instituted by Fateh Ali Shah, in honour of Sir John Malcolm, on his second mission to the Court of Persia in 1810, in company with Pottinger, Christie, Macdonald-Kinneir, Monteith, and other British officers, who rendered excellent service to Persia in organizing a body of her troops. These officers were followed by others, who in 1834, under Sir Henry Lyndsay Bethune, led the troops they had trained against the Pretenders who, on the death of Fateh Ali Shah, opposed the succession of the Vali Ahd (heir-apparent), Mohamed Shah, father of the late Sovereign. The Pretenders were defeated by Sir Lyndsay Bethune, and thus England established the stability of the throne of the Kajars in the direct line, and carried out the will of the great Fateh Ali Shah, who had appointed his grandson to succeed him after the death of his son, Abbas Mirza. During all the changes since Mohamed Shah's accession, Persia has always had reason to regard England as a friendly neighbour who has no aggressive designs against her. This feeling must have become conviction on finding that the defeat she suffered in 1856 caused her no loss of territory in the South, and the Order of the Lion and the Sun continues to be a signal sign of strong friendship between the two nations.

There are two great St. Bernard dogs belonging to the British Minister at Tehran, which, by their leonine appearance and tawny red colour, massive forms and large limbs, have made a remarkable impression on the imaginative Persian mind. They are dogs of long pedigree, being son and daughter of two famous class champions. Never being tied up, but allowed full freedom, they are perfectly quiet and good-natured, though at first sight, to the nervous, they may look doubtful, if not dangerous. These powerful giant dogs accompany the Minister's wife in her walks, and seem to know that they are to guard and protect; showy, gay Rex precedes, with his head up and eyes all about, while Dido follows, with head down, lioness-like, watchful and suspicious. Painful experience has taught the street-scavenger curs, which dash savagely at strange dogs, to slink away at the sight of this pair of champions, and the passers-by, who, as Mohammedans, are merciless to dogs, treat them as quite different from the dog they despise, so that they walk along feared and respected by all, man and dog alike. A Persian gentleman, riding past with his mounted followers, drew up at the sight of these St. Bernards, and said, 'I would give the finest Kerman shawl, or the very best Persian horse, for a puppy dog of that breed.'

Some of the mendicant dervishes of Tehran are of wild look, with matted locks, and with howling voice go about demanding, not begging, alms. They regard a giver as under some obligation to them, for affording him the means of observance of a duty imposed by religion. These stalk along defiantly, carrying club or axe, and often present a disagreeable appearance. One of them came suddenly by a side-path behind the Minister's wife, and followed, yelling out his cry of 'Hakk, hakk!' It was almost dark, and he did not see the great dogs, which had gone ahead. His cry and continued close-following steps were disturbing, so I turned and asked him either to go on at once or keep farther back. He frowned at what no doubt he considered my bad taste in objecting to his pleasing and superior presence, and hastened his pace a little to pass, but stopped suddenly on seeing the 'lion-dogs' belonging to the Janab-i-Khanum-i-Sifarat (the Lady Excellency of the Legation), and asked to be allowed to follow us, saying he would be perfectly quiet. On reaching the Legation gate, and seeing his way clear, the dogs having entered, he left, saying gently, 'Goodnight; God be with you.'

Formerly a lady could hardly walk about without some little fear of look or laugh calculated to annoy. This is often the case in a Mohammedan country, the meaning being that the figure and face should be shrouded and veiled. But in presence of Rex and Dido there is no sign of the light look or laugh; on the contrary, there is rather the respectful gesture of, 'The road is free to thee.' The vivid imagination of the Persian pictures the group as personifying the Imperial arms, the Lady with the Royal guard, the Lion of Iran.

Before the warriors of the Mehdi made the term 'dervish' better known, it was commonly understood to signify a beggar. But though the derivation is 'before the door,' yet this does not mean begging from door to door. The dervish originally was a disciple who freed himself from all family ties, and set forth without purse or scrip to tell of a new faith among a friendly people, and to tarry here or there as a welcome guest. In due course he developed into a regular soldier of the Church, and as schisms arose and the fires of religious animosities were kindled, various orders of fighting fanatics, calling themselves dervishes, sprang into existence. Such were the Ismailis, first known as the Hassanis, in Persia, in the eleventh century, similar in character to the present dervishes of the Soudan. In the more favourable sense of the word, the true dervishes of to-day in Persia represent the spiritual and mystic side of Islam, and there are several orders of such, with members who belong to the highest and wealthiest ranks.

In the time of Fateh Ali Shah, the mendicant dervishes, who were then as numerous and profligate in Persia as vagrant monks used to be in Spain and Italy, became such a pest that one of the first acts of his successor, Mahomed Shah, was to direct that no beggars should be tolerated except the lame, the sick, and the blind, and that all able-bodied men appearing in dervish garb were to be seized for military service. The profession fell out of fashion then, and there are now comparatively few mendicant dervishes to be seen. Those that still wear the 'ragged robe' do not all appear to follow the rules of poverty, self-denial, abstinence, and celibacy. One there was, a negro from 'darkest Africa,' who attached himself as a charity-pensioner to the British Legation in Tehran, and was to be seen in all weathers, snow and sunshine, fantastically dressed, chattering and chuckling in real Sambo style. He knew that his religious cry of 'Ya Hoo' was characteristic of him, and he was always ready to shout it out to the 'Ingleez,' whose generosity he had reason to appreciate. He had a story of being a prince of fallen fortune, who was kidnapped in Central Africa, traded and bartered across Arabia, and abandoned in North Persia. He was known as the Black Prince. During the cholera epidemic of 1892, he took up his residence under some shady chenar-trees of great age, a recognised resting-place for dervishes, close to the summer-quarters of the English Legation at Gulhek, in the vicinity of Tehran. One day he sat outside the gate and poured forth a pitiable tale of the death of his wife from cholera during the night, and begged for money to pay for her burial. Having made his collection, he disappeared at nightfall, leaving his dead partner under the chenar-trees, and it was then discovered that he had possessed two wives, who called him *agha*, or master, and he had departed with the survivor, leaving the other to be buried by strangers. After that he was known as the Prince of Darkness.

The privileged beggars or mendicant dervishes of Tehran are not all of the stained, soiled, dust-and-ashes description; some are occasionally seen presenting a pleasing contrast in washed white garments, and of neat appearance. There was one such in Tehran, a well-known cheerful old man, who looked as if he could, in quiet company, tell entertaining stones, for recitation is adopted by some of these wandering dervishes as a pleasant means of livelihood, and many of them in the storytelling art show considerable talent, cultivated taste, and retentive memory. But, to be successful, they must be able to indulge in variations of their old stories by the introduction of new incidents which they have heard or invented. One who is known for good style is always welcomed at the many tea-shops and gardens in village and town.

In a most unlikely spot, on a long stretch of sand in the Yezd Desert, I met a well-dressed dervish in clean, cool white clothes, who stopped on perceiving that I was a 'Firanghi,' and, gently swaying his neat dervish-dole dish, said quietly, 'Charity; alms are as dew-drops from the heavens,' a most appropriate speech in the sandy waterless waste. Membership with the higher dervish orders appears to signify and convey something of the character of Freemasonry. I know of one highly-placed Persian gentleman who is a dervish, and also of a European gentleman of Oriental light and learning who has been admitted to the same order. A famous Prime Minister of Persia in past time, Haji Mirza Aghasi, was a well-known but rather eccentric dervish. My knowledge of this was the means, on one occasion, of averting a disagreeable display of violence by a gay sort of madcap, the relative of a post-house master, who had attached himself as groom to the stable establishment. My smart Armenian servant, who was equally good as groom or table attendant, had taken off his warm pea-jacket to help in bracing up the loads on my baggage post-horses, which were to be driven loose at a canter, the usual practice when riding post with extra baggage. A powerful, merry-talking groom, who came forward with the horses, picked up the jacket and put it on, saying that the morning was cold. And so it was, for the month was November. When all was ready for a start, my servant asked him for the jacket, but the laughing *diwana*, or eccentric fellow, said it was a gift to him, and refused to part with it. Warm words passed, and I intervened and told him to drop his dervish ways and give back the jacket. The *diwana* became excited, and shouted to all who were standing by that I had called him a dervish, and had hurt his feelings badly. I then told him he was hard to please, as surely a High Vazir was good enough to be compared with, for was it not true that the famous Haji Mirza Aghasi was of the noble order of dervishes. He took in slowly what I said, then smiled, and gave back the jacket with a good grace. The Persians have a proverb similar to our own regarding giving to beggars, 'Avval khesh, baad darvesh' (First our own, then the beggar. Charity begins at home).

The ordinary Persian horses are small, but very wiry and enduring. In harness they are also capable of very long journeys in light draught, as proved in the carriage service between Tehran and Kasvin. The distance is about ninety-seven miles, divided into six stages. On arriving at one of these, I found that all the posting horses had been taken by a Russian Mohammedan merchant who was travelling ahead of me in great style, with five carriages. I had two vehicles, one a carriage for myself, and the other a *tarantass* for my servant and luggage, each drawn by three horses. There was considerable traffic on the road then, and the horses had only a few hours in the stable between 'turns.' It was night when I arrived at the post-house, and though anxious to go on, I had no option but to remain there till the horses should come back from the next stage. On their return, after three hours' rest and a feed of barley, six took my carriage and waggon to the next post-house, sixteen miles, where again I found an empty stable, the horses which had gone with the party ahead of me not having come back. On inquiring judiciously from the post-house master if the horses which had brought me from the last stage were able to do another, I was told that with an hour's rest and an extra feed they would be ready to go on. And they travelled the second stage well, showing no signs of distress. These horses had done sixteen miles in draught, and sixteen miles in cantering back to their stable during the evening and night; then thirty-two miles in draught with me in the morning, and after a short rest were to return the same distance to their own stable, all in double-quick time.

I had the privilege of again seeing what I consider one of the most interesting sights in Persia, the stables of his Majesty the Shah. They contain the very best blood in Asia, and comprise the pick of the finest horses in Arabia, Persia, Kurdistan, Karadagh, Khorasan, and the Turkoman country, also the choicest home-breds from the horse-farms belonging to the late Shah and his sons, the present Shah and the Zil-es-Sultan, all of them great horse fanciers and breeders. The late Shah had three breeding establishments: one in the vicinity of Tehran, another near Hamadan, and the third at Maragha, in Azerbaijan, where the pasture is good. In each of these there are said to be about one thousand mares and foals. There is no part of the establishment of a monarch of Persia to which more attention is paid than his horses. They are always placed under the care of an officer of high rank, who is styled Mir Akhor.

The Mir Akhor (Master of the Horse), Mohamed Hussein Mirza, a Prince of royal blood, shows by his intimate knowledge of the history of each horse, and the good condition of all and everything under his care, that he loves his charge well. We were first shown the racing-stud, called ***mal-i-shart*** (race-horses), thirteen in number, all in hard condition (the Persian expression is, 'as hard as marble'), and showing good bone and much muscle. They were Arabs, but not all imported from Arabia, some being bred from pure stock in the late Shah's establishments. The royal races are held at Doshan Tepe, six miles from Tehran, where there is a soft sand-soil course, said to be a two-mile one, but the correct measurement is one and a half miles. The Persians breed and train for long-distance speed and endurance, and the races at Doshan Tepe are from three to nine miles. The Prince pointed out the last winner of the nine-mile race, saying that he ran it in twenty-five minutes. This horse was a well-shaped, warm gray Arab, with black points. He, with a darker gray and a chestnut, all Arabs of pure breed from Nejd, none of which it is said can be obtained except by free gift, or rare capture in war, took the eye most with their make and shape. All were ridden slowly round the yard by their 'feather-weight' jockey-boys, dressed in red racing-jackets and blue breeches, with long, soft leather boots, and coloured handkerchiefs bound tightly round their heads in place of caps.

I think these *shart* horses in the royal stables, which are always kept in galloping-condition, are the outcome of the old days of flight or fight, when it was necessary to be always prepared for raid, attack, or treachery, and so often man's best friend in pressing need was his horse.

'A horse! a horse! my kingdom for a horse!'

After the racing stud came the riding-horses, sixty-two in all: deer-like Arabs of the best desert blood of Nejd and Anizah, and others of a stouter build from the country of the Jaf Kurds; selected cross-breeds from Persian and Turkish Kurdistan, and bigger-boned animals from the Karadagh, the result of a strong strain of good Northern blood. There were some long, low, powerful Yamut and other breeds from the Turkoman country, and some good-looking active small horses from Khorasan. From the Kashkai breeding-grounds near Shiraz were shown some fine big horses of high quality, also neat, stout mixed breeds from the hills and plains of Luristan and Persian Arabistan; and Arabs of the best type, bred from 'blood stock' by the Shah's sons, also choice specimens from the royal home farms.

Three gray Arabs, favourites of the late Shah, were brought out, set off with gold collars, and their points were gone over to show how powerfully safe they were as riding-horses on the hillside and the plain. One of them was said to be getting too old for good work, but he was bursting so with flesh and spirits that he threw out before and let out behind in such vigorous wide-circling style as to scatter the crowd of spectators, *gholams*, guards, and grooms. The most powerful and best-shaped among the riding-horses, in my opinion, were a Jaf (Kurd) dappled gray, and two big gray Turkomans, the latter very deep in the girth, and distinguished by the long, fine neck so common to their class, and rather large but lean heads, showing blood and breeding. The Turkomans say that the superior size and strength of their horses over others are due to the rich grass of their pasturelands, I may conclude this short account of the royal stud by mentioning that, as Persia is essentially a country of horses and horsemen, every foreign Minister on first arrival and presentation to the Shah receives the gift of a horse from his Majesty's stables. All these horses had their tails plaited or tied up. The Persians never cut a horse's tail, but tie it up, which not only improves the animal's appearance, but prevents the tail trailing on the ground, or being whisked about when wet or dirty, to the annoyance of the rider. The tail is only knotted up when the horse is made ready for riding, otherwise it remains loose, to be used for flipping off flies.

The stable of the King is deemed one of the most sacred of sanctuaries, and this usage continues in force to the present time. The stables of the foreign Legations are also regarded, by reason of the Ilchi-Envoy representative sovereign character, as affording a similar asylum, and in 1890 I was witness to protection being thus claimed in the stable of the British Minister. The military tribes of Persia have always regarded this sanctuary of the stable with the most superstitious reverence. 'A horse,' they say, 'will never bear him to victory by whom it is violated.' In a Persian MS. referred to by Malcolm, all the misfortunes of Nadir Mirza, the grandson of Nadir Shah, are attributed to his having violated the honour of the stable by putting to death a person who had taken refuge there. The same writer says that the fleeing criminal finds a place of safety at the head of the horse even when tied up in the open air; the fugitive touches the headstall, and is safe so long as he remains there. Malcolm again tells us of what is still observed, that it is not unusual for those of the military tribes who desire to show their respect at the funerals of chiefs and soldiers of high reputation to send a horse without a rider, but with arms upon the saddle, to swell the train of the mourning cavalcade. The favourite charger of the departed warrior, carrying his arms and clothes, accompanies the procession; the sheepskin cap he wore is placed on the pommel of his saddle; his scarf sash, or **kumarbund,** is bound round the horse's neck, and his boots are laid across the saddle. In all this may be seen the origin of similar customs now followed by the most civilized nations, and of the regard in which the horse is held as 'the noble animal.'

The late Shah had not a single English or European riding-horse in his stables, nor are any such seen in the country except some from Russia--heavy, coarse animals, bred in the Don districts, and used for carriage purposes. The artillery with the Persian Cossack brigade at Tehran also have a few Russian horses. Nasr-ed-Din had such a high appreciation of Arab and Eastern horses, of which he was in a position to get the very best, that he found it difficult to understand what he considered the fancy prices paid in England for racing stock. The story is told that when he was shown Ormonde at Eaton Hall, in 1889, and was informed that L14,000 had been offered for him, he tapped the ground briskly with his cane, and said in a vivacious manner: 'What! L14,000 offered for him? Sell him, sell him now to-day. Why, he may be dead to-morrow.' He would have been astonished to hear that Ormonde afterwards changed owners at the advanced price of about L30,000.

In speaking to two friends, competent judges of such matters, about the breeding and training for long-distance races in Persia, and the time in which it was said the nine miles had been run, I found that, while one thought the time might be reasonably correct, the other was more than doubtful. I have since then seen in the Journal of the United Service Institution of India, 1886, a paper on 'Horsebreeding in Central Asia, translated from the Russian of Kostenko by W.E.G.,' in which the following details regarding the Kirghiz race-meetings and the pace and staying powers of their horses are given. M. Kostenko mentions that the details are taken from an article by M. Garder in the Voyenni Sbornik for 1875. He says that among the Inner Kirghiz Horde, races for prizes were instituted by the Minister of State Domains, beginning with the year 1851. On October 4 of the same year a circular course measuring four miles was made, and the horses ran five times round it. The winner did the 20 miles in 48 minutes and 45 seconds. Commencing with 1853, the races were run over a distance of 13-1/3 miles on a circular course, and of these races detailed information from 1869 was obtained.

The greatest speed was recorded on October 2, 1853, when the distance (13-1/3 miles) was done in 27 minutes and 30 seconds. The longest time, on the other hand, was 39 minutes 30 seconds.

The Chief Administration of the State Studs did not credit the information sent from the Horde, so that in 1856 there was sent to the sitting committee a second metre, for the speed to be followed on it, the circumference of the circle having been previously measured. The president of the committee repotted that the measurement of the course was correct, except that in every 4 versts (2-2/3 miles) it was out 17-1/2 feet. The deficiency was then made good. Accordingly, on October 2 a trial was held, at which the speed was checked with the aid of the second metre that had been forwarded, and several watches with seconds-hands. These showed the 13-1/3 miles run in 31 minutes. Of nineteen races run over this course, the average time was 33 minutes 40 seconds.

In 1861 a race was run over another circular course, measuring about 3-1/2 miles, five times round. The mare that won performed the distance--about 17 miles--in 48 minutes 45 seconds. In the Kalmak *uluses* (groups of nomad tents) of the Astrachan Government, races of 10 miles have been held. The greatest speed recorded was in 1864, viz., 23 minutes 56 seconds; the longest time was in the same year, viz., 27 minutes. The average time between 1862 and 1865, and 1867 and 1869, was 25 minutes 15 seconds.

The riders in these races are lads of not more than ten or twelve years of age. They are in no way specially trained, as from early age they are always riding, and grow up in good condition for hard exercise. Their weights range from four to six stone.

The Persians are a nation of horsemen still, and most of them can ride well. All the migratory tribes breed horses, and such is the habit of observation of horses in the country, that, as a rule, a man is known by his horse, just as in some parts of England a man is known by his dog. Owing to the notice thus taken of a man's horse, a party of nomad brigands who carried off all my baggage-train in 1890 were discovered and hunted down. There is a road guard service for all the King's highways in Persia, and an annual fixed sum is allowed for its maintenance. Officials with influence among the neighbouring nomads farm this service on the main roads, and entertain a certain number of 'black-mail' men for each stage from the various tribal sections to keep watch and ward. The official who farms the road guard service is held liable to pay compensation for losses by robbery, and this stimulates the energies of all to recover stolen property and to keep the highways safe and secure. Incidents of robbery occasionally happen, but, all things considered, the system may be said to work fairly well, as instanced in the recovery of my baggage.

I had taken a short-cut over the hills to avoid some miles of circuit by the highroad, and on the way I met the relieved Governor of Luristan returning to Tehran, with a long train of well-guarded laden mules. Some little distance behind them came three mounted nomads, armed with Martini-Henry rifles (the common arm now in Persia), and showing well-filled cartridge belts. They rode up to me and my party, consisting of a *gholam* courier and two servants, all mounted. One of the nomads, riding a chestnut mare, while examining me intently, dropped a short stick which he carried, alongside of me, and on dismounting to pick it up, his mare wheeled round towards me, and I saw that she had lost her right eye. We passed on, and shortly rejoined the highroad, and when close to the next halting stage, a post-boy, driving three loose post-horses before him, galloped up to say that he had seen my baggage mules driven off the highroad by five armed nomads. The road guards were called, and on hearing my description of the three men we had met, and that one of them was riding a one-eyed chestnut mare, they at once said, 'Kara Beg and his sons are in this,' and rode off to follow the trail. Almost all my luggage was recovered that night, and Kara Beg was hunted hard, and disappeared. He had been suspected of several robberies carefully carried out, so that detection was difficult; but in my case it appeared that he had hung on to the rear of the Luristan Governor's baggage without being able to steal anything, and when disappointment had made his men sore and reckless, they followed up my mules, which had no guard, and carried them off. The tribal road guards knew where to find him and his men, and soon had most of the plundered property back. The recovery was due to identification of his mare.

The English national love of sport has lately introduced into Tehran the popular *gymkhana*, an institution which hails from India, where it is English enterprise under an Indian name. The British Legation has started this amusement, and it seems to provide energy for many who had longed for some fresh outdoor exercise, but could not organize it. Now, when weather permits, there are weekly gatherings for variety races, tent-pegging, and paper-chases. A very amusing and effective novelty, which I saw there for the first time, was a donkey tug-of-war. This new 'gym' was imported by a sporting young diplomatic secretary, who had lately arrived from Cairo, where he had seen it in full exercise. Tehran has excellent riding-donkeys for hire, well turned out, and attended by the usual smart-tongued youth. Eight donkeys, four a side, heading outwards, all ridden by Europeans, mostly English, were engaged in this sport. Neither whip nor spur was allowed. The rope was passed along under the right arm, and held as each rider thought best. At the word '*Off!*' heels were brought into fast play on the donkeys' ribs to make them move forward, and the scenes that followed were ludicrous and exciting. Riders were pulled off backward, and, still hanging on to the rope, they managed to remount and get again into the pulling line in time to drag off someone on the opposite side, who had lost his balance on the sudden 'go' forward from the lessened strain. This amusement was a highly popular one with the laughing spectators.

Our travelling-party on the outward journey had separated at Tehran, and I travelled back homeward alone. I left Tehran in the middle of November, and as there had been a heavy fall of snow some days before, I quite expected to have a cold crossing of the Kharzan Pass over the Elburz range. I did the journey to Kasvin comfortably in a carriage, and rode thence to Resht in three days. I was unexpectedly fortunate in finding that the bright weather had freed the road over the pass from snow, and I had a perfect day, with still air, for that part of my ride.

About halfway between Kasvin and Resht the road passes through the extensive olive-groves of Rudbar, which for many centuries has been the centre of a flourishing olive-oil and soap business. There are about sixty villages in the district engaged in this industry; they possess from eighty to one hundred thousand trees, each yielding on an average from six to nine pounds' weight of fruit a year. The olive as a fruit-tree has been known in Persia from a comparatively early period, and it is not surprising to hear the villagers ascribe quite a fabulous age to some of the old trees, just as in Italy some olives are credited with an equally astonishing antiquity.

To me it has appeared that the habit the olive has of sending up new stems from the root of an old trunk--just as the chenar sycamore does in Persia--may have made the old trees become young again, and thus present, to succeeding generations in the villages, the look of the same old trunks. Messrs. Kousis, Theophylactos and Co., of Baku, have obtained a concession for pressing and refining olive-oil in this district, and I observed the buildings which they are erecting for their business rising on the right bank of the river there.

Near Rudbar commences the thick growth of various hard-wood trees, which flourish well in the damp soil of the Caspian slopes and lowlands, and in November their foliage was surpassingly lovely, with many warm tints, from delicate red to deep russet and shades of shot-green and brown. On some of the high, thickly-wooded hills, the different colours ran in well-defined belts, showing where particular kinds of trees had found most favourable soil, and had grasped it to the exclusion of all others.

About forty miles from the Caspian coast I fell in with rain and mud--such mud as cannot be realized without being seen. I embarked at Enzelli on board a small Russian steamer, the *Tehran*, which had taken the place of one of the usual large vessels employed on the mail-service. The sea was rising as I embarked, and I was lucky in getting on board before the surf on the bar at the mouth of the lagoon became impassable. The steamer had five hundred tons of iron cargo on board, machinery for electric light and other purposes, intended for Tehran, but which could not be landed owing to the rolling sea. It was therefore carried back to Baku, a second time within a fortnight, for accident had prevented it being landed on the previous voyage.

There is always this risk of wind and weather preventing landing at Enzelli. Proposals have been made to remove the bar sufficiently to allow steamers of eight hundred tons to pass into the lagoon harbour; but the expense of doing this, and keeping up dredgers, would be great--too great, it is thought, to allow of any profitable return. The same landing difficulties are experienced at Astara and Lenkoran, the places of call between Enzelli and Baku. Should there be any intention of eventually making a railway from the coast to Kasvin and Hamadan, there to meet a line to Baghdad, then it would be the best course in every way to connect Resht with Baku by a railway along the coast, passing through Astara and Lenkoran.

The coast country is famous for its rice, which could be extensively cultivated, and the resources in forest and fishery produce are great. There would be considerable local traffic as the country opened up, and the through trade in oil from Baku would be a paying one. I believe the Russians know that it would be cheaper to build a railway along this coast-line of about three hundred miles, with such trade capabilities, than, in the absence of harbours, to erect breakwaters, make sheltered anchorages, and dredge navigation channels. For two-thirds of the distance the line would lie in Russian territory.

I met at Enzelli a foreign artist, whose acquaintance I had formed in Tehran, where he made some good pictures of local life and scenery. He was loud in his complaints of the elements--the heavy rain and the awful mud. He had come down the road with a minimum of travelling comforts, and had been rather miserable. On going off to the mail-boat in the steam-launch, he vented his feelings of disgust with Persia by spitting over the side towards the land, and saying, 'Ach! ach! what a country! 'May I never see it again!' When I reminded him of Tehran and its club, he acknowledged that he had enjoyed his stay there, and appreciated the place; but the rain and sea of mud at Resht had drowned and smothered all his pleasant memories of Persia.

The voyage to Baku was uneventful. There are two Astaras, one Persian, the other Russian, with the frontier stream between them. The steamer remained part of the night at the former place, and moved in the morning three miles to the anchorage opposite the latter. There the Russian Customs officers came on board to examine luggage. The first mate of the steamer, a Swedish Finn, attended the search proceedings, and became much interested In a rusty pistol which was found in the luggage of one of the deck passengers. The question arose, Was the pistol loaded? and he undertook to find out. He raised the hammer to full cock, and, placing the muzzle in his mouth, he blew down the barrel, with his finger on the cap nipple, to feel if the air passed through. He naively explained to me the certainty of this mode of discovering whether a percussion arm is loaded or not. In this instance the pistol was thought to be loaded, but it was found to be only choked with rust.

I had intended to return *via* Constantinople, but on arrival at Baku I learnt that the damage done to the railway between Tiflis and Batoum by a storm of unprecedented fury and unusually heavy floods was so extended and bad as to stop all traffic for a long time. I went to Oujari, a station one hundred and sixty miles from Baku, where I was hospitably entertained by Mr. Andrew Urquhart, a Scotch gentleman, established there with a factory and hydraulic presses for the liquorice-root industry, and from there I entered into telegraphic communication with Tiflis to ascertain if I could get a carriage to Vladikavkas, so as to join the railway and proceed home through Russia. There was such a number of passengers detained at Tiflis, en route to Batoum, and all anxious to go to Vladikavkas by road, that I found I should have to wait long for my turn. Accordingly, after six days' stay with my hospitable friend, I went back to Baku and took steamer to Petrovsk, whence I travelled by rail to Moscow and St. Petersburg on my way to England *via* Berlin.

A great petroleum field is now being developed near Grosnoje, a station on the Petrovsk Vladikavkas railway, north of the main Caucasus range; and an English company has had the good fortune, after venturing much, to find the fountain for which they and others have long looked. After carrying on 'sounding' operations for some time, and sinking several wells, oil was at length 'struck' towards the end of August at a depth of three hundred and fifty feet, and it came up with such force as to reach a height of five hundred feet above ground. The well was on a hillside, and the valley below had been dammed up previously to form a reservoir capable of holding a large supply of oil. But such was the flow from the fountain, that after a few days it rose above the dam, and, although every effort was made to raise and strengthen it, the oil overflowed, and the top of the dyke was carried away. Millions of gallons were lost, though on its course down the valley the oil completely filled another reservoir, which had been prepared for the oil of a rival company, but which never came from their own wells. Eventually the main flow of oil found its own level in a low-lying piece of ground, about four miles below the broken dam.

As the fountain continued to flow with almost undiminished vigour, the Governor of Grosnoje began to be alarmed at the damage which was being done by this deluge of oil, and he therefore placed four hundred soldiers at the disposal of the English engineer in charge, and by their organized labour he was able to repair the dam, so that the flow of oil was checked. A friend, from whom I received this account, visited the place on November 27, and saw the fountain still playing to a height of twenty feet, and also the lake of oil which had been formed. The lake was about three hundred and fifty yards long, one hundred and twenty yards wide, and from fifty to sixty feet deep. The fountain was still playing on January 10, but it shortly afterwards ceased to flow. The same company had another stroke of luck in again 'striking oil' last month at another spot, some little distance from the original fountain, while, strange to say, none of the other companies engaged in prospecting for oil there have as yet succeeded in getting so much as a gallon. All this flow of fortune to the one firm reads very like the luck of Gilead Beck in the 'Golden Butterfly.'

Mr. Stevens, H.B.M.'s Consul for the consular district of Batoum, shows in his report for 1894 that the demand for naphtha fuel is increasing in Russia at such a rate, owing to it being more and more widely adopted for railways, steamers, factories, and other undertakings using steam-power, that the time appears by no means far distant when the Russian home market may be in a position to consume in the shape of fuel almost the entire output of the wells of the Caspian, and he adds that probably the supply will even be insufficient to meet the demand. With all this in view, the value of the Grosnoje wells, situated as they are on the main line of railway through the heart of Russia, is likely to prove very great.

I landed in a heavy snowstorm at Petrovsk on November 30, and found the whole country under its winter sheet. Since October 1 all railway fares and charges in Russia have been greatly reduced, and the policy now appears to be to encourage travelling and traffic, which must result in a general improvement of the minds and condition of the people.

Railway travelling in Russia is now much cheaper than in any other country; a through first-class ticket from the Caspian to St. Petersburg, seventeen hundred miles, is but L4 10s., and the other classes are low in proportion. The carriages are comfortable, and the refreshment-rooms excellent.

With accurate information as to the sailings from Petrovsk to Baku and Enzelli, one can now go from London to Tehran in fourteen days. This, of course, means steady travelling, frequent changes, a saddle-seat for about one hundred miles (which can now be reduced to seventy-five), and some previous experience of rough life, so as to reconcile the traveller to the poor accommodation afforded in a Persian post-house. But the Russian road, now under construction, will soon change the rough ride into a fairly comfortable carriage-drive, with well-provided post-houses for food and rest.

CHAPTER VII.
THE SITUATION IN PERSIA (1896).
I.

--Shrine of Shah Abdul Azim --Death of Nasr-ed-Din Shah --Jemal-ed-Din in Tehran --Shiahs and Sunnis --Islam in Persia.

The famous shrine and sanctuary of Shah Abdul Azim, about five miles from Tehran, is a very popular place of pilgrimage with the inhabitants of the town, and its close neighbourhood to the crowded capital makes it a great holiday, as well as religious, resort. This shrine has been specially favoured by many sovereigns, and particularly by those of the present dynasty. On the Mohammedan special weekly day of prayer and mosque services, Friday, called Juma, or the day of the congregation, Shah Abdul Azim is visited by great numbers of people.

On Friday, May 1, this sanctuary was the scene of one of the saddest events which has ever happened in Persia--the murder within its sacred precincts of Nasr-ed-Din Shah, a monarch who was about to celebrate the jubilee of a reign which will always be remembered, not only for its remarkable length, but also for its peaceful character and general popularity. The proof of this popularity is that Nasr-ed-Din Shah was able to leave his country on three occasions for visits to Europe, and returned each time to receive a welcome from his subjects. This in itself is un-precedented in Eastern history.

I little thought when I had the honour of conversing with him in October last that it was possible that a King so admired and loved by his people, and then looking forward with pride and pleasure to the celebration of his approaching jubilee, should perish in their midst by the hand of an assassin within five days of the event.

Passing over what in the early years of his reign, through the exigencies of the times and the pitfalls of intrigue, led to the shedding of blood, we see in his later years a reluctance to inflict capital or severe punishment which almost amounted to a serious fault. I remember an instance of this in the case of a notorious highway robber, guilty of many murders, who was spared so long, that it was only on the bad effect of leniency becoming prominently dangerous to traders and travellers that the extreme penalty was sanctioned. I have already mentioned how the people had learnt to put their trust in the late Shah's desire to protect them against oppressive government in the provinces, and how he had made himself popular with the military and nomad tribes. The crime which has caused his death will undoubtedly be regarded as sacrilege, both with reference to the life which was taken and the sanctuary which it violated. And the abhorrence of the crime will strengthen what it was intended to end or weaken, viz., the influence and power of the Kajar dynasty. With the impressionable Persians there will be but one feeling, of shuddering horror that such a thing could be done by one of their own faith, who was a subject of their Sovereign.

A criminal of the deepest dye can abide with perfect impunity in the Mohammedan sanctuary, and the tranquillity of this sacred safety, we are told, brings reflection and repentance to work the redemption of many from evil ways. Thus we can understand how horror-struck the nation must be at the thought of the Shah being mortally wounded while in the pious act of kneeling in reverence on passing the chain which marks the actual line where the 'bast' or sanctuary begins.

The murder is said to have been prompted by the well-known agitator, Jemal-ed-Din, who, though called an Afghan, is really a native of Hamadan, in Western Persia; but having travelled and resided a short time in Afghanistan, the term 'Afghani' was added to his name. He was well known in Tehran in 1891 for his vehement and violent public speaking against all Western innovations. I have seen it stated that it was owing to him the tobacco monopoly was withdrawn, as he had roused the Moullas throughout Persia, and wellnigh brought about a revolution. Jemal-ed-Din no doubt took a strong part at Tehran in the agitation, but he was in no way such a prominent leader of it as has been represented. The sudden introduction of systematic labour and Excise regulations under foreign direction, by which it was said a few depots were to displace the numerous retail shops and stalls, at once created a hostile army of unemployed small owners of hereditary businesses, who worked on the fears and feelings of the mass of the people. The Moullas and guild-masters then took the lead, and brought about the cancelment of the concession. All this I have previously described. It suited well the nature of a stormy petrel like Je-mal-ed-Din to find himself in Tehran at that time, and he became an inflammatory public orator of the hottest kind. At first he confined himself to speaking against the tobacco monopoly and all European enterprise, and on his violent speeches being made the subject of some remonstrance, the Shah said that the Persians had long enjoyed great liberty of speech, and with them words generally took the place of deeds. But this freedom was misunderstood by Jemal, who gradually grew bolder, until his revolutionary utterances went beyond all endurance. He scarcely veiled his contempt for the Crown, and his opinion that all should combine to rid Persia of the rule of the Shah and the continuance of the Kajar dynasty. He was warned, but would not listen to reason; he was then arrested, and informed of the decision to deport him from Persia. On the day of his departure from Tehran under escort, he managed to make his escape, and took sanctuary in the same shrine of Shah Abdul Azim where the Shah was mortally wounded on May 1 by his follower, Mirza Mo-hamed Reza. Jemal opened negotiations with the Government from his asylum, and was finally persuaded to leave Persia quietly. It was said that he received generous treatment in the matter of his leaving, but I am aware that he stated he had cause for complaint on this head. We must bear in mind, however, that he was a hot hater of the Shah, and a thorough 'irreconcilable.' On quitting Persia he went to Constan-tinople, where he appeared to be allowed such free expression of disrespect to his Sovereign that the Shah addressed a remonstrance to the Sultan, who stated in reply that Jemal was leaving for some remote place to employ himself in literary work.

As a native of Hamadan, Jemal-ed-Din is a Persian subject; he is also of the Shiah faith, though it is believed that, in order to make things easy for himself, he passes as a Sunni where the State religion is of that creed. He was well received by the Shah on his visit to Tehran in 1890 as a man of learning and letters, and it is said that he accepted and enjoyed his hospitality. This, however, did not prevent him plotting against his royal host, and doing his utmost to compass the downfall of the Kajar dynasty. He probably saw clearly during his stay in Persia then that the Shah's authority rested too strongly in the minds of the people, by reason of his long and peaceful reign and mild rule, to give any hope of a successful revolution during his lifetime. And it may have been in this connection that recourse was had to assassination.

Jemal-ed-Din is credited among Orientals with a powerful energy and will in working on the enthusiasm of others, and establishing a moral despotism over them. His disciple, Mohamed Reza, appears to have resembled his teacher in reckless disregard of kindness, and determination to render evil for good. In him a willing hand was apparently found to carry out the first part of Jemal-ed-Din's programme for the reformation of Persia, but the possibility of madness in the act of murder was not foreseen. For the horror of the crime has been so intensified from being committed in the holy shrine of the sainted Shah Abdul Azim, that its object must be defeated in the most complete manner, and the reaction will result in stronger attachment to the throne of the Kajars.

Jemal-ed-Din held a brief for the union of Sunni and Shiah, an idea which from time to time has found favour with some advanced leaders of the former faith. He spoke of the gain to Islam in sinking their religious differences, and joining to form one Church and one creed. He was said to be very earnest on this point, and he succeeded in planting his opinions in Persia, as shown by the subject being still occasionally discussed. But the idea is entirely of foreign growth, and is generally introduced by enthusiasts like Jemal-ed-Din, who have exchanged their Persian national pride of Church and State for the ambition to see Islam ruling as one power from Constantinople to Pekin. These visionaries fail to see what thoughtful Persian politicians and Churchmen know well, that the Shiah schism has preserved Persia as a nation, for without it the incentive to popular cohesion would long ago have ceased.

The annual Passion-play to commemorate the murder and martyrdom of the progeny of Ali, and the solemn fast-days when their assassins are cursed and reviled, which are observed all over Persia, serve to keep alive their patriotism and pride of independence, for with the Persians, religion and patriotism are synonymous terms. There is probably no country where Church and State are more closely and fortunately bound together than Persia. Had the sovereignty not been Shiah, it would long ago have disappeared between its Sunni neighbours. With them the persecution of the 'accursed Rafizi,' as they speak of the sect, is the exercise of a holy duty, and their enslavement by Sunnis is a meritorious act, giving the heretics an opportunity of benefiting by example, and of rescue from perdition by conversion to the orthodox faith. Thus it was that the Hazaras and Shiah inhabitants of the small principalities on the head-waters of the Oxus were sold into Sunni slavery, and the purchase of the Shiah Circassians in the Turkish markets was justified on the same grounds. The bitter experience of ages has taught all Shiahs that, once helplessly at the mercy of the Sunnis, there must be absolute submission on all points. This conviction has buried itself deep in the minds of the Persian people, and they now and then are painfully reminded of the savage readiness of their Sunni neighbours to emphasize the fact.

In 1892 a bazaar quarrel in Herat between Sunni and Shiah traders grew to a disturbance, and culminated in some of the latter, Persian subjects, being slain and their goods plundered, the Moullas solemnly pronouncing their judgment that it was 'lawful' for Sunnis to take the lives as well as the property of the heretical Shiahs. The Shah, on the representation of the Meshed religious authorities, addressed a remonstrance to the Amir Abdul Rahman Khan, who, being a strong and wise ruler, made reparation. The religious antagonism is very bitter in Afghanistan, and were it not for the warlike character and good fighting qualities of the Shiah Kizzilbash tribe at Kabul, their presence at the capital would not be tolerated by the bigoted Moullas. The common danger makes the Kizzilbashes a united band and dangerous foe, and arms them to be always ready to fight for their lives. They have become a power which it is the policy of the rulers to conciliate, and thus secure their support. But notwithstanding this, the fanatical hatred of the orthodox Sunni, as representing both Church and State, cannot be suppressed. I was with General Sir William Mansfield (the late Lord Sandhurst) when he, being Commander-in-Chief in India, had a conversation with the Amir Sher Ali of Kabul on general subjects, in the course of which the Amir, in rather a captious manner, made some sharp remarks on what he called the hostile differences in the Christian Church; Sir William rejoined by referring to the great division in Islam between Sunni and Shiah, and asked if there were many of the latter faith at Kabul. A look of displeasure passed over Sher Ali's face as, half turning towards his people who stood behind him, he said, in a severe tone, 'Yes, there are a few of the dogs there, sons of burnt fathers.'

The mutual hatred ever existing with Sunni and Shiah has always worked against very cordial relations between Turkey and Persia, and once certainly, in the sixteenth century, the fear of Persia, then actively hostile on the south-eastern border, benefited Austria and Russia by deterring the Turkish Power, in the days of its triumph and strength, from extended aggressive operations north and west of Constantinople. Accordingly, the reconciliation of Sunni and Shiah has long been a cardinal point of policy with the Porte. While it appears that Austria thus benefited in an indirect manner through Turkey's fear of Persia, it is an interesting coincidence that, from the time the latter extended her diplomatic relations beyond those with Russia and England, which, for a considerable period, were the only Western Powers represented at the Shah's Court, Austria has held a prominently friendly position in Persia. Austrian officers have long been employed in her army, and the fact of the Emperor Francis Joseph and the late Shah Nasr-ed-Din having ascended their thrones within three months of each other in the same year (1848) was regarded by the latter as an association with himself of the highest honour and amity. And this brings to my recollection a matter connected with the Austrian Legation at Tehran which occurred after the deportation of Jemal-ed-Din in 1891. Mohamed Reza, the murderer of the late Shah, remained in Tehran, and continued the treasonable practices which had been originated by Jemal, even to the extent of disseminating his revolutionary opinions by means of printed papers.

The press used for printing was a lithographic one, and one of the Mirzas employed by the Austrian Legation having been drawn into Jemal's secret society, he was induced to set it up in his own house. The usual informer accomplice was found, or offered himself, for the purpose of betraying his brethren, and the police became so keen on capture that oblivious of the privilege enjoyed by the employe of a foreign Legation, they entered the Mirza's house and arrested him in the act of printing treasonable papers from the lithographic press. The Mirza was carried off to prison before the Minister knew of the occurrence, but, on being informed, he promptly made a strong remonstrance against the violation of international privilege. The fullest satisfaction was at once given; the Chief of Police called and apologized, and the prisoner was released and sent to the Legation.

The Minister conducted his own inquiry, and on undeniable proof of the truth of what was alleged, he dismissed the Mirza from his post, and the Persian authorities were then free to arrest him. The Mirza was kept a prisoner for some time, and was eventually released with Mohamed Reza and his companions. The Tehran telegram of May 4 tells us that Mohamed Reza continued his old course of public hostility to the Government, and was again imprisoned, but once more obtained his release, and was granted a pension by the Shah, notwithstanding which he remained discontented, as the 'black-mailer' generally does, greed suggesting that the price paid for silence is inadequate. This lenient treatment of the conspirators was quite characteristic of the later disposition of Nasr-ed-Din Shah, and his averseness to judicial severity.

From what is now known regarding the Mohammedan revival and Church union contemplated by Jemal-ed-Din, it is obvious that the idea of any connection between Babism and the crime at Shah Abdul Azim is out of the question, for the Babis of Persia and Jemal-ed-Din's followers have little or nothing in common. I have already told how the former are averse to violent measures, practise no public preaching, and suffer in silence, while the latter we know shout aloud and try to terrorize.

When Nadir Shah accepted the throne, he insisted on the abandonment of the Shiah schism and reunion with the Sunni faith, and he went to extreme lengths in suppressing the unwillingness of the clergy to accept the arbitrary decree which he issued in proclaiming his mandate. His attempt to bridge the great gulf between the hostile creeds entirely failed, and the Persians remained Shiahs. Freedom of thought and liberty of speech are national characteristics and privileges, and with minds never thoroughly subjected to severe Church discipline, the people have been ever ready to indulge in free criticisms on religious and other matters. They had no desire to study a new religion, even at the command of their King, and, judging that any change would be irksome, they sided with the Moullas, and without display refused to be Sunnis. Nadir's devotion to ambition was greater than his love of religion, and his object in trying to drive all into one creed was to remove the obstacles to the progress of his Imperial power among the Sunnis of India, Afghanistan, Central Asia, and Asia Minor. On issuing his mandate to form the Shiahs into a new branch of the true faith, he intimated to the Emperor of Constantinople his high aim at general concord among Mohammedans.

Islam, as it was forced on Persia, was the faith of foreign conquerors and oppressors, so it never has had the same considerable influence on the people as elsewhere. This, taken with their habits of freedom of thought and love of romance and poetry, inclined them to champion the Shiah schism, which, on the fall of the Arab power, they adopted for their National Church. I refer to this in connection with what is now reported of Jemal-ed-Din's relations with the chiefs of the State Church party at Constantinople, for in his preachings in Persia there were clear signs of movement towards a great Mohammedan revival, which was to restore Islam to its old dominant position in the world.

CHAPTER VIII.
THE SITUATION IN PERSIA (1896).
II.

--The Shah Mozuffer-ed-Din --His previous position at Tabriz --Character and disposition --His sons --Accession to the throne --Previous accessions in the Kajar Dynasty --Regalia and crown jewels --Position of the late Shah's two sons,   Zil-es-Sultan and Naib-es-Sultaneh --The Sadr Azem (Grand Vazir) --Prompt action on the death of the late Shah.

Among the great families of Tartary from whom the chiefs of the royal Kajar tribe claim descent, much importance has always been given to the birth of the mother of a candidate for high position. Therefore, in the choice of an heir to the throne, Persia, as now represented by the Kajar dynasty, looks to the claims of the mother as well as the father, and requires royal birth on both sides. For this reason Mozuffer-ed-Din Mirza, the second son of the late Shah, his mother being a Kajar Princess, was preferred to the first-born, Sultan Masud Mirza, known as the Zil-es-Sultan. It has been customary with the Kajars to have the Vali Ahd, or Heir-apparent, at a distance from the capital, and for him to be nominal Governor-General of Azerbaijan, the richest and most important province of Persia. Its capital is Tabriz, a town of considerable commercial prosperity, through its Russian and other foreign trade connections. The mother of Mozuffer-ed-Din Mirza maintained a dignified position of high influence at the Court of the late Shah until her death, which took place at Tehran in May, 1892. During the intrigues and disquieting rumours which at one time prevailed, the strong influence of the mother of Mozuffer-ed-Din Mirza was always present to watch over his interests in the Shah's palace, and when she died his friends feared that he had lost his only good protector. But the Sadr Azem, then known as the Amin-es-Sultan, rightly interpreting the true feelings of the royal father and the people, promptly filled the vacancy himself, and has now led the nation to act as executors of the will of the departed Shah in securing the peaceful succession of the heir whom he appointed.

There has been much speculation regarding the character, abilities, and disposition of Mozuffer-ed-Din Shah. I think the general opinion formed of him by those who have had opportunity of judging is favourable. He is of kindly disposition, and has pleasing manners, and though prudence has demanded that as Heir-apparent he should not take a very active part in public affairs, yet there have been occasions on which he showed himself to be a capable ruler. His position made it absolutely necessary that he should avoid all appearance of impatience of subjection to the Central Government, and he showed considerable tact in never giving cause for suspicion on this point. He was most successful in keeping clear of everything that could offend the susceptibilities of his royal father, and was always regarded as a dutiful son and a loyal subject. His was a most difficult position to fill, and the fact that he filled it to the satisfaction of the Shah proves that he possesses the qualities of prudence, patience, and good judgment.

Mozuffer-ed-Din Mirza had with him for a long time as Kaimakam, or Vazir, the well-known Amir-i-Nizam, who was virtually Governor-General of Azerbaijan, for the Shah held him personally responsible for the administration of the province. He was a man of strong character, and had great influence in Azerbaijan. His wealth also added to his importance, and it was not surprising, perhaps, that he considered himself qualified to hold independent opinions. The active resistance to the tobacco monopoly was first shown in Tabriz, and he was said to have encouraged opposition to the wishes of the Central Government. In consequence of this the Shah summoned him to Tehran in the end of 1891, and early in 1892 appointed him to be Governor-General of Kurdistan and Kermanshah, a post which he still holds. On this change taking place, Mozuffer-ed-Din was directed to assume responsible charge of the Northern province, and has continued to exercise it till now. The Amir-i-Nizam was succeeded as Kaimakam by Haji Mirza Abdul Rahim, who was formerly Persian Minister at St. Petersburg, and as his predecessor had been Minister at Paris for some years, the European experiences of these able Vazirs no doubt aided the further education of the Vali Ahd. The association of enlightened companions and Ministers gave him opportunities of gaining knowledge which not only informed him on matters of public importance and general interest, but was also calculated to prepare him for the position of Sovereign. It has been said of him that he is entirely Russian in his inclinations, and considering his long residence at Tabriz, within view, as it were, of the great power of Russia's vast empire, it would be strange if he had not been strongly impressed with the vital necessity of secur-ing the goodwill of the Czar, and we may feel certain that the advice and opinions of the two Vazirs I have mentioned were to this effect. But it does not follow that Mozuffer-ed-Din Shah's mind is wholly bent in that one direction. Judging from the present as well as the past, he knows well he can believe in England's sincere desire to preserve the same friendly relations with him as existed with his father, and that she wishes to see Persia strong, prosperous, and independent.

While the Amir-i-Nizam was at Tabriz, his energetic management left noth-ing for the Prince to do, and as, moreover, a policy of caution debarred him from taking a very active part in public affairs, he occupied himself chiefly with the simple amusements of a country gentleman. He was greatly interested in his horse-breeding farms established on the fine pasturelands of Maragha, near Lake Urumia, and made frequent visits there. He is a good horseman and a keen sportsman with gun, rifle, and falcon, just as his father was, and his love of life in the open brought him much in contact with the people in a manner that developed the good-nature for which he is known. He possesses in a large measure the pleasing characteristics of a nomad chief, and on the departure of the Amir-i-Nizam, his personal qualities, added to the sympathetic exercise of his duties, made his rule popular.

While his prominent brothers have benefited pecuniarily to a considerable ex-tent by the positions which they hold, the Vali Ahd was content to maintain a miniature Court on a modest scale, keeping up his dignity in a fitting manner, and showing no desire to amass money. The people were aware of this, and respected him for not taking advantage of his opportunities to enrich himself as others might have done. More than once lately mention has been made in the papers of the large fortune which the Zil-es-Sultan is said to have acquired at Isfahan, and invested in foreign securities.

Mention may here be made of the first two sons of Mozuffer-ed-Din Shah. The elder is Mohamed Ali Mirza, twenty-four years of age, whose mother is a daughter of Mirza Taki Khan, Amir-el-Kebir and his wife, who was the favourite sister of the late Shah. The second is Malik Mansur, about fifteen years of age, whose mother is a daughter of Ismail Mirza, a Prince of the reigning Kajar family. The latter is spoken of as an engaging and bright-looking youth, and is generally believed to be the favourite son. The other sons are not much known nor mentioned as yet, but it may be said that the succession in the direct line appears to be well assured.

Naturally the health of the Heir-apparent was a matter of great consequence to himself, in the first place in view of his future, and secondly to those who desired to see the nomination to the succession undisturbed, for change would have produced great uncertainty and unrest throughout the country. When I visited Tabriz in the end of 1892, there were three physicians attached to the Vali Ahd's Court. One was the Hakim Bashi, Mirza Mahmud Khan, a Persian of superior education and professional training, who was in constant attendance on the Prince, and with him were associated the English Dr. Adcock (who had then been four years in Tabriz, and is still with Mozuffer-ed-Din Shah), and an Italian doctor, S. Castaldi, brother of the wife of the Russian Consul-General, regarding whom I have no late information.

The succession of Mozuffer-ed-Din Shah so far has been peaceful, notwithstanding the fears of many that opposition would appear in the South. This is the first time with the present dynasty that on the death of the Shah the Vali Ahd has found no rival in his path. Curzon stated very decidedly in his important work on Persia that a contest for the throne was most improbable, and his forecast has proved correct. Mozuffer-ed-Din Shah is the fifth Sovereign of the Kajar dynasty, which was founded by Agha Mohamed Shah, and I may here remark that the reign of the late Shah was just within one year of completing a century of royal rule shared by only three successive sovereigns of this line, a notable fact in an Oriental kingdom.

Fateh Ali Shah succeeded to the throne in 1797, having been appointed Vali Ahd by his uncle, Agha Mohamed Shah, who had no family of his own. He was the son of Hussein Kuli Khan (full brother of the Shah), Governor-General at Shiraz, and he was there with his father when called to the throne at Tehran. On the death of Agha Mohamed Shah in camp with his army on the Northern frontier, General Sadik Khan, chief of the Shekaki tribe in Azerbaijan, seized the opportunity to gain possession of the Crown jewels and treasure, and quitted the camp with his men; but the rest of the troops marched at the command of the strong Prime Minister Haji Ibrahim, to the capital, which by his orders was held by the Kajar chief, Mirza Mohamed Khan, for the legitimate heir of the Shah. Two competitors for the Crown appeared in the South, in the persons of Fateh Ali Shah's own father, and a son of Zaki Khan Zend; but both, as well as the Shekaki chief who advanced similar claims in the North, and Nadir Mirza, grandson of the great Nadir Shah, who had entered Khorasan from Afghanistan, and raised the standard of revolt, were soon defeated and driven into submission. The Shakaki chief was able from his possession of the Crown jewels and treasure to make terms for pardon and preferment; but he afterwards broke his oath of allegiance, and rebelled. He was captured and confined in a dungeon, where his life soon ceased.

Fateh Ali Shah died in 1834, and was succeeded by his grandson, Mohamed Shah, son of the capable Abbas Mirza, who predeceased his father. He was at Tabriz, holding the post of nominal Governor-General of Azerbaijan, which was the customary position assigned to the Vali Abd, when his grandfather died, and I have in a previous chapter told of the part taken by British officers in defeating the Pretenders, who attempted to dispute his right to the throne. These Pretenders were his uncles Ali Mirza, the Zil-es-Sultan, and Hussein Ali Mirza, Governor-General at Shiraz, each of whom proclaimed himself King. Fateh Ali Shah died at Isfahan while on his way to Shiraz to compel the obedience of his son Hussein Ali Mirza, who in expectation of his father's death from age and infirmity had decided to withhold payment of revenue to the Crown. The rebellious son advanced with an army, and took possession of the jewels and treasure which his father had brought with him; and his brother, the Zil-es-Sultan, seized what had been left at Tehran, but Mohamed Shah afterwards regained possession of the whole.

Nasr-ed-Din, son and heir-apparent of Mohamed Shah, was present at his post of Governor-General of Azerbaijan when his father died in Tehran, and there was an interval of disturbance for the six or seven weeks which passed between the death of the one King and the coronation of the other. During this period revolution prevailed in the towns, and robbery and violence in the country. The son of

Ali Mirza, the Zil-es-Sultan, the Prince-Governor of Tehran, who had disputed the succession of Mohamed Shah, issued forth from his retirement in Kasvin to contest the Crown with his cousin; but the attempt came to an inglorious end. A revolt at Meshed with a similar object also failed, and then Mirza Taki Khan, Amir-i-Nizam, proceeded successfully to consolidate the power of Nasr-ed-Din Shah, whose long reign, and on the whole good rule, have so accustomed the people to peace that the old ways of revolution and revolt on the death of a Shah have been forgotten and changed.

The regalia and Crown jewels of Persia mentioned in these changes of royal rule have, by inexplicable good fortune, been preserved from plunder while in the hands of rebels. The Crown jewels are in great part a portion of the splendid spoil which Nadir Shah obtained in the sack of Delhi, when it was the capital of the richest empire in the East. On his assassination near Meshed, the treasury was seized by the troops, and while a considerable share, including the famous Koh-i-Nur diamond, which now adorns the English crown, fell to the Afghans with Nadir's army, the greater part, with the Koh-i-Nur companion diamond, known as the Darya-i-Nur (Sea of Light), was secured by Persian soldiers, who hid it all away in Khorasan and the adjoining districts.

When Agha Mohamed Shah found leisure from his wars and work of firmly establishing his authority, he turned his attention to the recovery of Nadirs jewels, and proceeded to Meshed, where, by means of cunning and cruelty, he succeeded in wresting from the plunderers of Nadir's camp, and others, the rare collection of gems and ornaments now in the royal treasury at Tehran. The value of the collection is believed to be very great.

The singular preservation of the regalia and Crown jewels of Persia from plunder while they were in the hands of rebels after the death of Agha Mohamed Shah, and again on the death of Fatch Ali Shah, is most remarkable. A superstitious feeling of fear and respect appears to have kept them from being lost from the Crown, or it may be that, on the principle of 'safety in numbers,' every one, with a prospective share of the plunder in view, was a check on his neighbour against theft of that which they thought belonged to all.

Sultan Masud Mirza, better known as the Zil-es-Sultan, the eldest son of the late Shah, has generally been regarded as likely to challenge the right of his younger brother to the throne. His ambition and overweening self-confidence combined to make him imprudent in permitting his partisans to speak aloud of his superior qualifications as a successor to his father. The late Shah's considerate treatment of him on all occasions also led him to make ill-judged requests for such extended rule in the South that his father said Persia was not large enough for two Shahs. I think his idea of a viceroyalty in the South came from foolish vanity, and not from any serious thought of semi-independence, as some who heard him speak on this subject supposed.

His father always wrote to him as 'my well-beloved first-born,' and up to 1888 he allowed him great power and freedom of action. He was fond of 'playing at soldiers,' and he went to work at this amusement with such energy and will that he formed a numerous and very efficient army under well-trained officers, too good, the Shah thought, to be quite safe. Nasr-ed-Din sent an officer whom he could trust to Isfahan to bring back a true report on the army there; and such was the Zil's self-assurance, that he went out of his way to show him everything, and to make the most of his force.

The Shah, on learning all, became jealous or suspicious, and ordered the reduction of the troops to the moderate limits really required for provincial purposes. As affairs then stood, the Zil, with his well-appointed army, was master of the situation, but he was constrained to submit. He singled out the Amin-es-Sultan (now the Sadr Azem) as his enemy at Court, and regarded him as the strong adviser who influenced the Shah. His relations with Tehran then became so strained that the Shah summoned him to his presence to have his wishes clearly explained to him. The meeting of father and son did not tend to smooth matters, and the latter, allowing his temper to carry him to extreme lengths, tendered his resignation of the various governments he held, asking only to retain the governorship of Isfahan. His request was granted, and from that time he made no secret of his enmity to the Prime Minister.

Two or three years later the Shah restored to him some of the provinces which he had resigned in 1888, and this enabled, him to carry out more successfully the task which he had set himself, viz., that of amassing money, after his army was broken up. The warlike Bakhtiari tribe form the most important part of the military strength under the nominal command of the Zil-es-Sultan, but he alienated them entirely by his cruel and treacherous murder of their popular chief, Hussein Kuli Khan, in 1882, and the long imprisonment of his son, the equally popular Isfendiar Khan. Now that he has promised allegiance to his brother, Mozuffer-ed-Din Shah, we may regard the peace of the South as assured.

The Naib-es-Sultaneh, Kamran Mirza, as Minister of War, Commander-in-Chief, and Governor of Tehran, who was in constant attendance on his father, was also regarded by foolish partisans as a likely successor to the throne, but he himself never entertained the idea. His position as head of the army gives him no real power--in fact, it rather takes from his influence as Governor of Tehran; for the soldiers look upon him as a costly appendage, for whose pleasures and palaces their pay is clipped.

There is really no standing army, in Persia as we understand such, except the royal guard and the weak Persian Cossack brigade at Tehran. The artillery and infantry which do all the garrison work are militia regiments, embodied for two years at a time. The conditions are one year's service to two years' leave, and that they serve under their own local chiefs and officers. The administration of regiments is given to Ministers, high officials, and others for purposes of emolument or distinction, as the case may be. This system gives the influence over the troops to those who deal with their pay, and not to the Commander-in-Chief, who is regarded merely as the keeper of the great gate through which the pay passes after toll is taken. The Naib-es-Sultaneh, equally with his brother, the Zil-es-Sultan, appears to have a great dislike to the Prime Minister, whose loyalty to the Sovereign and his heir could not fail to create strong jealousy in high places.

I shall now finish with a few remarks on the able and sagacious Sadr Azem, the Prime Minister, who, by his strong character, resolute will, and prompt action, has proved his loyalty to the Crown and his fidelity to the Shah. He became Prime Minister at an unusually early age for such a high position, and this preferment drew upon him the jealousy and envy of many in such a manner as often to cause him great embarrassment. There can be no doubt of his conspicuous energy and talent. His pleasing manner and happy disposition attract adherents and gain for him their best services. In addition to his personal qualities, he has an astonishing knowledge of public affairs, which makes him a most valuable Minister. With the people he is deservedly popular, for not only is he liberal and kind, but he understands their feelings and can interpret their minds.

He was beside Nasr-ed-Din Shah in the shrine of Shah Abdul Azim when the assassination took place, and at once brought his Majesty back to the palace in Tehran. This happened about two o'clock in the afternoon, and the Shah breathed his last within four hours afterwards. It appears that the Sadr Azem immediately grasped the situation, and put himself in telegraphic communication with the Vali Ahd at Tabriz, four hundred miles distant. He then summoned all the Ministers, State officials, military commanders, and the most influential people of the city, to the palace, and announced the death of the Shah. Under his able guidance, the prompt recognition of Mozuffer-ed-Din Mirza as Shah, in accordance with the will of his father, was effected.

The English and Russian Legations, as representing the two strongest and chiefly interested European Powers, were immediately informed, and the Minister of the former, and the Charge d'Affaires of the latter, were invited to the palace. On their arrival, the Sadr Azem wired to the Vali Ahd in their presence the allegiance of the whole party who were there assembled. This was done about four or five hours after the death of Nasr-ed-Din Shah, and the following morning, in consequence of this decisive action, Mozuffer-ed-Din was publicly proclaimed Shah of Persia.

Thus the electric telegraph, which Nasr-ed-Din Shah introduced into Persia, has been the means of helping most materially to save the country from the uncertainty which has hitherto always produced revolution and civil war in the interval between the death of one Shah and the accession of his successor.

THE END.

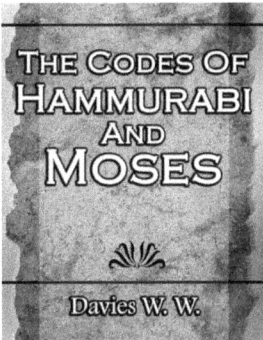

The Codes Of Hammurabi And Moses
W. W. Davies

QTY

The discovery of the Hammurabi Code is one of the greatest achievements of archaeology, and is of paramount interest, not only to the student of the Bible, but also to all those interested in ancient history...

Religion   ISBN: *1-59462-338-4*   **Pages:132**
MSRP $12.95

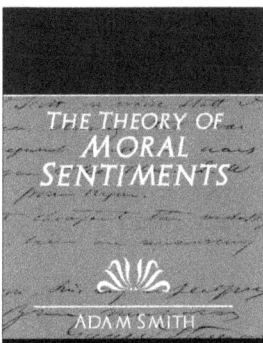

The Theory of Moral Sentiments
Adam Smith

QTY

This work from 1749. contains original theories of conscience amd moral judgment and it is the foundation for systemof morals.

Philosophy ISBN: *1-59462-777-0*   **Pages:536**
MSRP $19.95

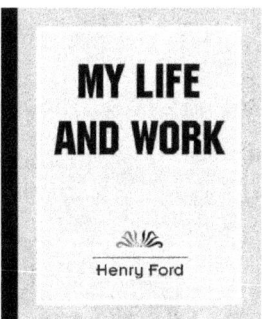

Jessica's First Prayer
Hesba Stretton

QTY

In a screened and secluded corner of one of the many railway-bridges which span the streets of London there could be seen a few years ago, from five o'clock every morning until half past eight, a tidily set-out coffee-stall, consisting of a trestle and board, upon which stood two large tin cans, with a small fire of charcoal burning under each so as to keep the coffee boiling during the early hours of the morning when the work-people were thronging into the city on their way to their daily toil...

Pages:84

Childrens   ISBN: *1-59462-373-2*   *MSRP $9.95*

My Life and Work
Henry Ford

QTY

Henry Ford revolutionized the world with his implementation of mass production for the Model T automobile. Gain valuable business insight into his life and work with his own auto-biography... "We have only started on our development of our country we have not as yet, with all our talk of wonderful progress, done more than scratch the surface. The progress has been wonderful enough but..."

Pages:300

Biographies/   ISBN: *1-59462-198-5*   *MSRP $21.95*

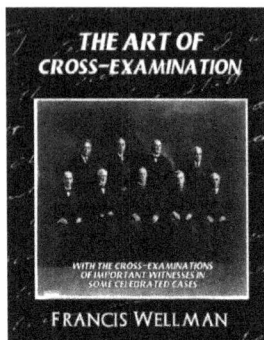

The Art of Cross-Examination
Francis Wellman

QTY

I presume it is the experience of every author, after his first book is published upon an important subject, to be almost overwhelmed with a wealth of ideas and illustrations which could readily have been included in his book, and which to his own mind, at least, seem to make a second edition inevitable. Such certainly was the case with me; and when the first edition had reached its sixth impression in five months, I rejoiced to learn that it seemed to my publishers that the book had met with a sufficiently favorable reception to justify a second and considerably enlarged edition. ...

Pages:412

Reference   **ISBN:** *1-59462-647-2*   *MSRP $19.95*

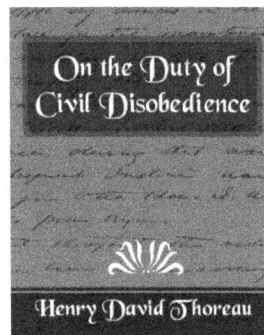

On the Duty of Civil Disobedience
Henry David Thoreau

QTY

Thoreau wrote his famous essay, On the Duty of Civil Disobedience, as a protest against an unjust but popular war and the immoral but popular institution of slave-owning. He did more than write—he declined to pay his taxes, and was hauled off to gaol in consequence. Who can say how much this refusal of his hastened the end of the war and of slavery ?

Law   **ISBN:** *1-59462-747-9*   **Pages:48**

MSRP $7.45

Dream Psychology Psychoanalysis for Beginners
Sigmund Freud

QTY

Sigmund Freud, born Sigismund Schlomo Freud (May 6, 1856 - September 23, 1939), was a Jewish-Austrian neurologist and psychiatrist who co-founded the psychoanalytic school of psychology. Freud is best known for his theories of the unconscious mind, especially involving the mechanism of repression; his redefinition of sexual desire as mobile and directed towards a wide variety of objects; and his therapeutic techniques, especially his understanding of transference in the therapeutic relationship and the presumed value of dreams as sources of insight into unconscious desires.

Pages:196

Psychology   **ISBN:** *1-59462-905-6*   *MSRP $15.45*

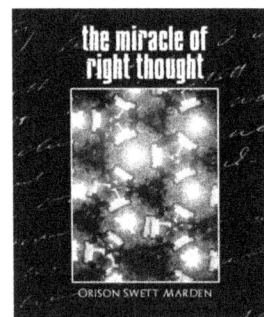

The Miracle of Right Thought
Orison Swett Marden

QTY

Believe with all of your heart that you will do what you were made to do. When the mind has once formed the habit of holding cheerful, happy, prosperous pictures, it will not be easy to form the opposite habit. It does not matter how improbable or how far away this realization may see, or how dark the prospects may be, if we visualize them as best we can, as vividly as possible, hold tenaciously to them and vigorously struggle to attain them, they will gradually become actualized, realized in the life. But a desire, a longing without endeavor, a yearning abandoned or held indifferently will vanish without realization.

Pages:360

Self Help   **ISBN:** *1-59462-644-8*   *MSRP $25.45*

QTY

The Rosicrucian Cosmo-Conception Mystic Christianity *by Max Heindel*   ISBN: *1-59462-188-8* **$38.95**
The Rosicrucian Cosmo-conception is not dogmatic, neither does it appeal to any other authority than the reason of the student. It is; not controversial, but is: sent forth in the, hope that it may help to clear...   New Age/Religion Pages 646

Abandonment To Divine Providence *by Jean-Pierre de Caussade*   ISBN: *1-59462-228-0* **$25.95**
"The Rev. Jean Pierre de Caussade was one of the most remarkable spiritual writers of the Society of Jesus in France in the 18th Century. His death took place at Toulouse in 1751. His works have gone through many editions and have been republished...   Inspirational/Religion Pages 400

Mental Chemistry *by Charles Haanel*   ISBN: *1-59462-192-6* **$23.95**
Mental Chemistry allows the change of material conditions by combining and appropriately utilizing the power of the mind. Much like applied chemistry creates something new and unique out of careful combinations of chemicals the mastery of mental chemistry...   New Age Pages 354

The Letters of Robert Browning and Elizabeth Barret Barrett 1845-1846 vol II   ISBN: *1-59462-193-4* **$35.95**
by Robert Browning and Elizabeth Barrett   Biographies Pages 596

Gleanings In Genesis (volume I) *by Arthur W. Pink*   ISBN: *1-59462-130-6* **$27.45**
Appropriately has Genesis been termed "the seed plot of the Bible" for in it we have, in germ form, almost all of the great doctrines which are afterwards fully developed in the books of Scripture which follow...   Religion/Inspirational Pages 420

The Master Key *by L. W. de Laurence*   ISBN: *1-59462-001-6* **$30.95**
In no branch of human knowledge has there been a more lively increase of the spirit of research during the past few years than in the study of Psychology, Concentration and Mental Discipline. The requests for authentic lessons in Thought Control, Mental Discipline and...   New Age/Business Pages 422

The Lesser Key Of Solomon Goetia *by L. W. de Laurence*   ISBN: *1-59462-092-X* **$9.95**
This translation of the first book of the "Lernegton" which is now for the first time made accessible to students of Talismanic Magic was done, after careful collation and edition, from numerous Ancient Manuscripts in Hebrew, Latin, and French...   New Age/Occult Pages 92

Rubaiyat Of Omar Khayyam *by Edward Fitzgerald*   ISBN: *1-59462-332-5* **$13.95**
Edward Fitzgerald, whom the world has already learned, in spite of his own efforts to remain within the shadow of anonymity, to look upon as one of the rarest poets of the century, was born at Bredfield, in Suffolk, on the 31st of March, 1809. He was the third son of John Purcell...   Music Pages 172

Ancient Law *by Henry Maine*   ISBN: *1-59462-128-4* **$29.95**
The chief object of the following pages is to indicate some of the earliest ideas of mankind, as they are reflected in Ancient Law, and to point out the relation of those ideas to modern thought.   Religion/History Pages 452

Far-Away Stories *by William J. Locke*   ISBN: *1-59462-129-2* **$19.45**
"Good wine needs no bush, but a collection of mixed vintages does. And this book is just such a collection. Some of the stories I do not want to remain buried for ever in the museum files of dead magazine-numbers an author's not unpardonable vanity..."   Fiction Pages 272

Life of David Crockett *by David Crockett*   ISBN: *1-59462-250-7* **$27.45**
"Colonel David Crockett was one of the most remarkable men of the times in which he lived. Born in humble life, but gifted with a strong will, an indomitable courage, and unremitting perseverance...   Biographies/New Age Pages 424

Lip-Reading *by Edward Nitchie*   ISBN: *1-59462-206-X* **$25.95**
Edward B. Nitchie, founder of the New York School for the Hard of Hearing, now the Nitchie School of Lip-Reading, Inc, wrote "LIP-READING Principles and Practice". The development and perfecting of this meritorious work on lip-reading was an undertaking...   How-to Pages 400

A Handbook of Suggestive Therapeutics, Applied Hypnotism, Psychic Science   ISBN: *1-59462-214-0* **$24.95**
by Henry Munro   Health/New Age/Health/Self-help Pages 376

A Doll's House: and Two Other Plays *by Henrik Ibsen*   ISBN: *1-59462-112-8* **$19.95**
Henrik Ibsen created this classic when in revolutionary 1848 Rome. Introducing some striking concepts in playwriting for the realist genre, this play has been studied the world over.   Fiction/Classics/Plays 308

The Light of Asia *by sir Edwin Arnold*   ISBN: *1-59462-204-3* **$13.95**
In this poetic masterpiece, Edwin Arnold describes the life and teachings of Buddha. The man who was to become known as Buddha to the world was born as Prince Gautama of India but he rejected the worldly riches and abandoned the reigns of power when...   Religion/History/Biographies Pages 170

The Complete Works of Guy de Maupassant *by Guy de Maupassant*   ISBN: *1-59462-157-8* **$16.95**
"For days and days, nights and nights, I had dreamed of that first kiss which was to consecrate our engagement, and I knew not on what spot I should put my lips..."   Fiction/Classics Pages 240

The Art of Cross-Examination *by Francis L. Wellman*   ISBN: *1-59462-309-5* **$26.95**
Written by a renowned trial lawyer, Wellman imparts his experience and uses case studies to explain how to use psychology to extract desired information through questioning.   How-to/Science/Reference Pages 408

Answered or Unanswered? *by Louisa Vaughan*   ISBN: *1-59462-248-5* **$10.95**
Miracles of Faith in China   Religion Pages 112

The Edinburgh Lectures on Mental Science (1909) *by Thomas*   ISBN: *1-59462-008-3* **$11.95**
This book contains the substance of a course of lectures recently given by the writer in the Queen Street Hall, Edinburgh. Its purpose is to indicate the Natural Principles governing the relation between Mental Action and Material Conditions...   New Age/Psychology Pages 148

Ayesha *by H. Rider Haggard*   ISBN: *1-59462-301-5* **$24.95**
Verily and indeed it is the unexpected that happens! Probably if there was one person upon the earth from whom the Editor of this, and of a certain previous history, did not expect to hear again...   Classics Pages 380

Ayala's Angel *by Anthony Trollope*   ISBN: *1-59462-352-X* **$29.95**
The two girls were both pretty, but Lucy who was twenty-one who supposed to be simple and comparatively unattractive, whereas Ayala was credited, as her Bombwhat romantic name might show, with poetic charm and a taste for romance. Ayala when her father died was nineteen...   Fiction Pages 484

The American Commonwealth *by James Bryce*   ISBN: *1-59462-286-8* **$34.45**
An interpretation of American democratic political theory. It examines political mechanics and society from the perspective of Scotsman James Bryce   Politics Pages 572

Stories of the Pilgrims *by Margaret P. Pumphrey*   ISBN: *1-59462-116-0* **$17.95**
This book explores pilgrims religious oppression in England as well as their escape to Holland and eventual crossing to America on the Mayflower, and their early days in New England...   History Pages 268

QTY

The Fasting Cure *by Sinclair Upton*   **ISBN:** *1-59462-222-1*   **$13.95**
In the Cosmopolitan Magazine for May, 1910, and in the Contemporary Review (London) for April, 1910, I published an article dealing with my experiences in fasting. I have written a great many magazine articles, but never one which attracted so much attention...   New Age/Self Help/Health Pages 164

Hebrew Astrology *by Sepharial*   **ISBN:** *1-59462-308-2*   **$13.45**
In these days of advanced thinking it is a matter of common observation that we have left many of the old landmarks behind and that we are now pressing forward to greater heights and to a wider horizon than that which represented the mind-content of our progenitors...   Astrology Pages 144

Thought Vibration or The Law of Attraction in the Thought World   **ISBN:** *1-59462-127-6*   **$12.95**
by William Walker Atkinson   Psychology/Religion Pages 144

Optimism *by Helen Keller*   **ISBN:** *1-59462-108-X*   **$15.95**
Helen Keller was blind, deaf, and mute since 19 months old, yet famously learned how to overcome these handicaps, communicate with the world, and spread her lectures promoting optimism. An inspiring read for everyone...   Biographies/Inspirational Pages 84

Sara Crewe *by Frances Burnett*   **ISBN:** *1-59462-360-0*   **$9.45**
In the first place, Miss Minchin lived in London. Her home was a large, dull, tall one, in a large, dull square, where all the houses were alike, and all the sparrows were alike, and where all the door-knockers made the same heavy sound...   Childrens/Classic Pages 88

The Autobiography of Benjamin Franklin *by Benjamin Franklin*   **ISBN:** *1-59462-135-7*   **$24.95**
The Autobiography of Benjamin Franklin has probably been more extensively read than any other American historical work, and no other book of its kind has had such ups and downs of fortune. Franklin lived for many years in England, where he was agent...   Biographies/History Pages 332

Name	
Email	
Telephone	
Address	
City, State ZIP	

☐ **Credit Card**   ☐ **Check / Money Order**

Credit Card Number	
Expiration Date	
Signature	

Please Mail to: Book Jungle
PO Box 2226
Champaign, IL 61825
or Fax to: 630-214-0564

ORDERING INFORMATION

web: *www.bookjungle.com*
email: *sales@bookjungle.com*
fax: *630-214-0564*
mail: *Book Jungle PO Box 2226 Champaign, IL 61825*
or PayPal *to sales@bookjungle.com*

Please contact us for bulk discounts

DIRECT-ORDER TERMS

**20% Discount if You Order
Two or More Books**
Free Domestic Shipping!
Accepted: Master Card, Visa,
Discover, American Express